The Real G   ~~ape

A Diary of West Bromwich Albion's
Season 2004 - 05

By
Stefan Langford and Gavin Shepherd

ISBN: 0-9545874-1-3

The authors wish to thank the following people for their help with the writing of this book:

Vince - you know
Andy Smith
Paul Smith
Aunty Pauline/Mom
H
Danny Boy
Pete Webb
Malc
Swoff

and Fay and Katy of course, for putting up with all the travel, mood swings and listening skills x

Published by
Stefan Langford and Gavin Shepherd
c/o. 24 Elm Croft
Oldbury
West Midlands
enquiries to albionbook@hotmail.com

Printed by Juma, Sheffield
Tel: 0114 272 0915   Fax: 278 6550   Email: juma@btconnect.com

Blackburn away

So here we are again. It seems like only yesterday me and Gav had our wigs on that sunny afternoon two years ago at the end of our first Premier adventure. To be fair, time has flown by and my beloved Baggies are now back in the top flight of English football. We made it as runners-up to the unfancied Norwich City and were never out of the top two all season. It was strange to be honest because most of the media and people you spoke to in the street had us down for promotion from the word go and so it proved, but ask any Albion fan about backing us and being let down and they will tell you a story. We were actually promoted at the home game with Bradford, well in fact it was before the kick off as Sunderland failed to beat Wigan in the morning game. I was elated and the afternoon was a typical sunny, flag waving celebration like you've seen so many times on the TV at other clubs, but to say it was better or indeed, as good as that monumental last day cliff hanger two years ago would be untrue. I began to question whether trips to Anfield, Stamford Bridge and St James's Park would still hold the magic and anticipated excitement like they did so amazingly last time out. Without doubt my experience of Premiership football two years ago was one from the heart that left me with starry eyes and a "little boy in the sweet shop" sense of place. Would it be the same? Would I actually have expectations above being on the same pitch as the big boys? These were the emotions that pulled at me over the remaining weeks of the season.

The close season is a surreal time of the year. It is a time of total nonsense in the papers, outrageous speculation based on absolutely nothing and meaningless friendlies, eventually. I spent the summer reading (well scanning) weeks worth of articles all discussing Patrick Vieira's guaranteed move to Real Madrid. His wages, house (mansion), debut opponents, endorsement deals, kit to be worn, role in the team, contractual arrangements, his first paella, etc. Each time, the language used in the article was so conclusive there could be no doubt he was going to Spain. Newspapers make me laugh at this time of the year they are as useful as Sven's half time team talks. Needless to say Vieira pledged his future to Arsenal and the comics went after somebody else to make a story out of. Their favourite word when discussing a player and transfers is "linked". In my experience this word at this time of the year translates to "hasn't even heard of the club". Talking of transfers we did actually spend some money this summer, whether it will be enough to keep us in the division only time will tell but fair play. Anyway, Smithy said he would drive to Lancashire as I drove here last time …. Glad he can remember because I certainly couldn't. Vince also had a ticket because of a mix up at the ticket office (surely you're joking) but I can't go into that because it will greatly reduce the chances of having this book on sale in the club shop. The five of us headed up the M6 and picked the bones out of England's 2004 European Championship failure – Sven bore the brunt of most points raised. 10.30am services. Now last time out it became quite clear that our match day diet was not exactly in agreement with the British Medical Society's idea of healthy eating. So that said, I had a full English with an Oasis fruit juice. It was the same services where I had met that Italian leather trader if you remember. I looked around but couldn't see our European neighbour, perhaps he's made enough to open a boutique or maybe he's just been caught.

We arrived in the former mill town at midday and reached The Fernhurst soon after parking. Plenty of Albion were already here and I reminisced for a minute, thinking about all those referees, flags and banners and that giraffe. Burg rang me at about 12.30, he and Smithy were in Crewe, I said "son, we're not playing Crewe". He then went on to tell me about a four hour train journey that took in some interesting places and involved a good number of trains. You can't trust British Rail son, leaves on the track and all that. Burg was in New Street at a quarter to 8 this morning but the girl refused to sell him beer till 8am then she found out her clock was fast so he had to wait even longer. Smithy wasn't wearing a cap either so had to keep going to the toilet to check his hair. They met up with us at about 2 to tell the tale. The pub was full of Albion and that tingling feeling you get when you haven't been to a game for ages crept up on me. Talking of excitement, poor old Vince had been awake since 6am thinking of the game. Don't tell me football doesn't get you. We reached our seats in the upper tier in time for kick off but Paul was about four seats away on the same row and Vince twenty rows away! I called him over about ten minutes in as there was a spare seat behind me, Andy and Gav.

The Baggies took close on 4000 fans while I was left bemused by the empty seats in the Blackburn sections – first home game and all that. We controlled the first half I'm not joking, with the defence looking solid. Greening looked hungry and assured but Clement and Johnson in the centre of midfield didn't quite look the part (Clement is our left back!). The front two worked hard with new boy Kanu (his first name is Nwankwo so most people prefer to refer to him by his surname for some reason) showing some outrageous skill. On the half our mark Horsefield was brought down and Clement stepped up to take the free kick. He hammered it into the wall, it took a deflection of sorts and rifled past Uncle Sam in goal to put us one up. We went wild. The Albion section exploded and me and the lads joined the other 4000 in letting everyone know…..that "The West Brom are back, The West Brom are back". The second half reminded me of recent England internationals at major championships. We played in red and white, sat back and defended for 45mins and inevitably got caught. A huge cross swung over and Short challenged Robinson for the ball. I'm not sure who got the decisive touch but it nestled into the corner of Hoult's net for 1 – 1. Oh well, it finished the same score after hanging on for the last ten minutes and we had our first point on the board (Wolves were here last season in their opening fixture and got beat 5).

We trudged back to the car and headed down the motorway quite content with our first half performance anyway. We stopped at the services so Paul could have his third burger of the day and got back in reasonable time to make cheese and biscuits at The Wernley courtesy of Swoff's wife Lil. She did point out, however, that I was not to have the pig's pudding as some bloke had helped his self and spat all over the lot in the process! Villa at home next week, needless to say I've got stomach ache already.

Aston Villa home

So here we are first home match of the season and it's our "friends" from Aston in their claret and blue. After checking the obvious fixtures, like who have we got first and last and when do we go to Old Trafford, you normally find yourself looking down the list for the old enemy. (A few years ago it would have been those Dingles from the custard bowl but as they can't get their act together these days, we keep changing places – which was nice!)

The original old enemy for the 25+ year old Albion fan are obviously the Villa and we didn't have to look far for the first meeting of the season. Now as this game is so early in the season both teams will be wanting to get a good start under their belts as well as taking a few points off their local rivals.

During a few beers in the Wernley on the Friday night before the big game, Mr John Swoffer Senior had been having a laugh with us, as usual, trying to persuade us we didn't stand a chance and that Vassel and Cole would be all over us from the kick-off. We'll see how long his grin lasts tomorrow night if we beat them, sorry, when we beat them – bit of optimism please, new season, new players – Kanuuuuuuuu! Anyway, Swoff said he was going for a pre-match drink in the Navigation Inn in Bridge Street and we would be welcome to join him.

Match day morning and we're off to have a drink in the pub which we have passed every home game and slaughtered it on each occasion due to the fact that a) it never looks open, b) it hasn't seen a coat of paint in probably 20 years, and c) it looks like it's going to collapse at any moment, apart from that it doesn't look too bad! We park up in the usual spot and walk back towards the pub, how do we get in, what sort of people drink here, will we get out again – all sorts of questions going through our minds. Now to make matters slightly worse, we've got Vince (Rob Harris – don't ask why Vince. There really is no explanation – honestly) with us for the home game this season and if he comes within 50 yards of a Burberry cap, he starts going home – not one for violence you see, like the rest of us really. Round the pub, through a virtually flattened fence and through a dodgy back door entrance in through the kitchens or something!

Once inside it was much of the same really, curtains drawn – no wonder it always looks closed, hardly any lights on. To be honest I think there was more light coming from the fridges behind the bar than anywhere else. Pint of lager two quid, glass of lemonade pound – as you'd expect, but to charge a pound for a glass of water which the bloke behind the bar had poured out of a two-litre bottle of Volvic was taking the piss slightly, especially as he had just told us we could have the whole bottle for a pound. Daylight robbery, I say!

Over towards Mr Swoffer and who else should be in there apart from Swoff senior? Big Mart, Gurp, Richie Stevens, young Swoff, Dearny, Big Craig, Macca, George Caswell and Cyril and their mate who winds the Smith twins up with his constant moaning all through the game. In the end we were glad we had ventured into uncharted territory, took the plunge, and had a drink in what must be the worst looking pub in Smethwick. But the strangest thing to happen before we left for the ground at approximately 12:05pm was when one of the owners climbed along all the chairs and opened the curtains. You know how these landlords like to make an extra bit of money now and again, early opening – naughty naughty!

As we queue up to get through the turnstiles, the banter is already in full flow.

"Chim Chimeny, Chim Chimeny,

Chim Chim Cherrue,

We hate those b******s in claret and blue!"

Unfortunately for some of the visiting fans who have picked up tickets at the ground, the gate between the two sets of supporters is shut (obviously!), these fans have now got a half hour walk to get 20 yards from where they are standing – ah, what a shame!

The game starts with the two sets of teams walking across the pitch for a line-up in front of the East Stand and then a hand-shaking session. Hello! Are we at an international game or something? And more to the point, why is Megson wearing shirt and tie again? I assumed it must have been some first game of the season ruling at Blackburn last week. I just hope someone's got the necessary gadgets for when Meggo has a H.A. during the game because he's popped a vein in his neck or something.

The game starts at the usual hectic pace of a derby, and as it's the first home game it just adds to the atmosphere. Kanu is applauded for ever touch, flick, pass, dribble, fart, cough, burp, and even gets a standing ovation when his passes go astray or straight out of play. Let's just give him man of the match now, or even player of the season – it's only the second game but everyone loves him. Look, just put him on the mural-thing and we can get on with things.

Greening, Purse, and Scimeca seem to be settling in well, but it was one of the better players from last season who gave Villa their first real chance. A clumsy challenge out wide gave Hitzlsperger the opportunity to send a ball into the Baggies box. Mellberg jumped highest to guide the ball past the oncoming Hoult. Shit marking, silly goal to give away really and so early. 4 minutes gone and we're one nil down!

From then on it was chances all round really. Cole fired a shot across the face of Houlty's goal, fortunately no one was closing in on it. Kanu's 18-yarder clipped off Laursen and flew inches over. Hoult then kept out a Gareth Barry effort from close range and with the help of Robinson then managed to prevent the ball crossing the line after the Hitzlsperger-Mellberg combination had beaten Albion's defence again. I'd just like to thank the FA for deciding that today's game would be officiated with a linesman from the QAC Blind School in Harborne. Robinson's leg appeared to be so far behind the line that he was probably directing traffic on the Birmingham Road with his big toe!

Clement soon came close for the Baggies after collecting a lay off from Kanu, as his strike went just wide. Kanu's magic nearly provided Horsefield with his first goal but Sorenson saved at point blank range. Then Laursen bundled over the Horse as he attacked the inside right channel, and to the delight of the home fans, the ref awarded a free kick. "About bloody time too ref, thank you very much! He's only been fouling him all day!" From the resulting Greening cross, Clement rose unchallenged to plant his header in the near corner. Get in!!!

Second half saw much of the same. Plenty of chances for both sides surprisingly coming mainly from free kicks and corners! Purse was closest to opening his West Brom account – no, Dave not another customer for the branch – with two headed efforts from respective corners. Purse had to be at his best at the other end as Cole was proving to be more of a handful as the game progressed. Enter Zoltan Gera, Hungarian captain, who provided an inch perfect ball through the Villa defence for Horsefield to run onto. As Action Man Hansen would say, "…his first touch let him down….", and Sorensen was able to prevent an Albion second. Still more attacks as the last few minutes approached and I think Gavin McCann must have forgotten which sport he was playing. He decided to take up circus skills for the final moments of the second half and gave us a quick demo in juggling. Fortunately for us he was standing in his own penalty area at the time, but unfortunately that linesman from the blind school had brought his mate along to ref the closing stages of the game and just as Villa's claims were turned away in the first half, so were the appeals from the Albion players, coaching staff, and fans alike. Miss of the day was almost given to the Horse for his one-on-one effort but his blushes were saved when Johnson had a last minute shot deflected into the air inside the Villa box, he continued his run but completely miss-timed his volley with the ball bouncing between his legs and then his shot going past the far post from only a few yards out.

As Stef said the other day, AJ is fast becoming the "nearly-man" of the Albion. Nearly scoring, nearly playing the perfect pass, nearly getting a tackle in, nearly intercepting a pass, nearly holding a regular Wales place down (but when you've got Koumas and Savage above you, you can't grumble), but you can always expect 110% commitment from him every game even if he is feeling the effect in the latter stages. Keep going Jonno – you'll score an absolute screamer one of these days!

One – one, final score. Honours even. Everyone happy-ish! They had a disallowed goal (but if the ref says it wasn't a goal......) and we should have had a penalty.

Spurs on Wednesday. The inevitable insults hurled at Robbie Keane and him coming on to score the winning goal – we'll see....... ?

Tottenham Hotspur home

After the excitement of the Navigation we thought we'd better slow things down a little with a pre-match pint and fodder Wernley-style. Carling and curry all round, then off to our usual car park space. Vince is working nights this week so we've got the pleasure of everyone's favourite Scouse – Peter Jones. I think Scouse managed to watch all but three or four games at home last season and went to a few away games. Not bad considering he didn't have a home or away season ticket!

This evening's game is the second game in four days and we've got Everton on Saturday. Who plans these fixtures? Anyway, on with tonight's game. "All hail Zoltan Gera!" He may not have mastered much English since he arrived but if you let your feet do the talking you don't need to say anything! After some silky touches when he came on towards the end of the Villa game, I think Mr Haas knew where he was going to be at the start of this game! He's done well but you can't keep this kind of talent on the bench "in case you need to change a game".

The best way to change a game is to start well and this kid really showed us what he is made of in the third minute.

Scimeca returned a defensive clearance back towards the Tottenham area where our new Hungarian hero controlled the ball as it fell over his right shoulder with the outside of his foot, held off a challenge and two strides later rifled the ball past Robinson at the near post. One nil up after 3 minutes – Burg and Smithy have definitely missed that goal! Probably just getting in their taxi from the Chapel or somewhere.

More fancy footwork from Kanu (Kanuuuuuuuu Kanuuuuuuuu – sorry, I must stop this childish immorality but he is good though) enabling Horsefield a very good shooting chance which would have beaten Robinson if it wasn't for the recovery by England new-boy Ledley King. AJ gave the ball away to Kanoute who advanced and then pulled the ball back into space where the Baggies defence thankfully cleared their lines. As Albion wasted possession, Spurs took more hold of the game and Redknapp and Mendes were able to set up further chances for their proven strikers. Defoe's best chance came after Robinson gave away the ball after Spurs had cleared an Albion corner. His deflected shot hitting the side netting. Then a double save from Hoult, first stopping a long range effort before reacting quicker than anyone else when Defoe was ready to pounce on the loose ball. You could tell it was coming really and ten minutes or so before half-time Defoe linked up with Kanoute and sent the ball past Hoult, who should have done a lot better, into the back of the net.

Then just before the break, Kanu opened his scoring records for the Baggies, well it look alright from where I was sitting and according to everyone around us, it looked good enough to them! Gera crossed from the right allowing Kanu to strike at goal, his shot hit the post, Johnson hit the rebound straight at Robinson and as the ball came back to earth, Kanu swivelled and acrobatically sent the ball over the line. Much jumping, shouting and screamin, and standing up on seats (Stef). Now I know it was a bit of a scramble but what's the lineman flagging for now? Disallowed! Much protesting and arm waving by Kanu and Horsefield but to no avail. Offside?? Offside my arse!

Second half started with another lapse in concentration from our Robinson, allowing Redknapp to slot in Defoe. His shot beat Hoult but not the upright. "Robbo, get a grip mate! You're meant to be setting an example as captain aren't you?" Then from almost the same position Hoult's reflex save prevented Davis from scoring from an unmarked midfield position. Horsefield thought he'd won a penalty when more good work by Kanu and Greening had sent him through on goal. No such luck from the man in the middle though! More end to end action as both teams tired and settled for a draw.

Megson changed Johnson for Dyer with twenty to go or so, but even though he tried, his pace wasn't winning the day for Albion on this occasion. Some right-backs this season, I am sure, will keep Mr Dyer in their pockets if he gets more chances to play, but there will be some games where he could turn out to be a great asset to have on the bench when players start to tire.

Final whistle of the evening brings the proceedings to another stalemate conclusion. That's three games played and three games drawn. Some would say we still haven't won and some will be pleased to point out we're still unbeaten!

Now about this disallowed Kanu goal! On this occasion we have to hold our hands up, take back those few moments of anger, hatred, bitterness and rage and apologise to the man with the flag. After viewing the highlights on Central Sport Special (Now there's a blast from the past! Waiting up till about half midnight to see highlights of a midweek defeat away at Grimsby or somewhere and finding out that we lost 3-0, played really shit and now all they're going to show is the actual result. Thanks!), sorry I keep forgetting we're Premiership now aren't we, I mean Match of the Day, I think that Kanu and Horsefield were offside when Gera crossed the ball – only just offside though!

Everton next, without their boy-wonder Rooney! He's still injured but he'll probably have signed for Newcastle or someone by then.

Everton away

I put my tent up at Stourport on the Friday afternoon knowing that the only chance of getting on the site Bank holiday weekend was to be there early. You see, Everton away right in the middle was not ideal. Me and the lads planned to come back from the game and head straight for the campsite Saturday night. Anyway, I set the tent up with Fay's help and everything was sorted. Gav was going to his second long distance wedding in a week (that is serious brownie points to call upon at a later date) so Vince had his ticket. Saturday morning and Vince picked me up at 9.30 before going round to get Andy and Paul. We headed for the M6 and discussed a number of points including Kanu's much needed strike partner and Wayne Rooney (not the same point by the way). We stopped at the services for the usual good value, high quality breakfast (surely by now you're smiling slightly). I had a traditional English for 6 quid then spotted what I thought was dog food in a bowl next to the dried out beans. "What's that?!!" I said pointing to the steaming turd and the old lady behind the counter replied "Corned beef hash, it's part of a set meal you can't have any". That's a shame I thought, then as I was about to leave the counter she called me back, "There you go me duck" she said handing me this side plate of reddy brown, greasy smeg, "Try that and if you like it next time your in, (motorway service!!) you can have it then". I looked at her and thought, "Have you gone temporarily insane love?" For the record I did try a bit and it was quite tasty but the fact that most of the potato and meat was actually floating put me off a little.

We parked on the huge carpark at the edge of Stanley Park and headed for The Arkle outside Anfield. We came here last time so knew it was okay. The pub was empty really but it was only 12.30. Some Albion were already there and this one particular idiot made it his business to walk around in a woolly hat singing and being loud and awkward with the bar staff. He wanted everyone to know he was there - you know the a-holes I'm talking about. The pub soon filled up and he quietened down to a squeak. Scouse rang us at about 1.30 telling us he was at Lime Street and on his way to meet us. He walked in at about 2.15 and I immediately shouted "Scouse, Scouse" when Vince went "Don't, son". I thought that's a bit out of order, not wanting to call Scouse over after knowing him all your life and that, then I realised how I must have looked. In a pub, outside Anfield, in Liverpool, shouting "Scouse" as loud as you like - was it me Vince was worried about or poor old Scouse amongst a load of Albion? I'm not sure.

Scouse had come on the train and it reminded me of a little journey me, Gav and the Smiths made last year to Forest. Burg, Smithy and two of their mates invited us to go to Forest on the train. We got the 126 from Burg's and arrived in New Street with loads of Albion for a 10 o'clock train. When we got to Nottingham we got off to be met by loads of Police. They were sifting through the fans and sending some to wait on the side, whilst allowing others up the stairs. My angelic face saw me through the security and Gav and the Smiths soon followed but as we turned round there was Burg and Smithy with his cap, standing on the side with the other hooligans in tow. The Police marched them up the stairs and when we met them a copper turned and said "You with these?" to which I said yes, so off we all traipsed. Now for some this might be a regular occurrence but to me, Gav and the Smiths it was a real experience. We were marched along the road by 20 coppers and 4 riot vans. When I asked where we were going I was told straight - a pub. We got to this pub which looked condemned to me and filled it. The Police stood on the front and back doors and fire exit not allowing anyone in or out. The pub didn't serve food but it did have Sky TV. After about an hour the others in the pub were becoming restless. Chanting started of an anti-IRA nature and the Fruit machine was smashed for its pound coins. Some bloke stuck chewing over the CCTV camera then proceeded to set fire to a newspaper so as to set the fire alarm off - he succeeded but the Police still wouldn't let us out. Paul went to the Police on the door and asked if we could leave as we wanted food but he was told to go back and have another drink. He said he had had enough lager to which a WPC quipped "have a whiskey then!" At about 1.45pm we were rounded up on the back Car Park (I'm not joking) because the pub had run out of lager. We were then marched almost in single file whilst one copper held a video camera in each of our faces towards another pub. At this point me, Gav and the Smiths were losing patience with our hosts and the hooligan element we found ourselves caught up with. The police were simply not interested in listening to us as we asked to leave the group. As we crossed the river I began talking about the drainage basin of the Trent as loud as I could so the nearest copper would hear in the hope that he would think I was sane. As we passed the ground one officer finally broke and escorted us to a burger stall and then to the turnstile. I have never seen anything like it in my life. Rounded up, herded along and spoken to like idiots - needless to say I don't think I'll be going on the train again.

Anyway back to Everton, we got in the ground and made our way to our seats - lower tier this time after the awful view from the back of the upper tier last time round. We were in the corner close to the home section behind the goal. Albion were basically unchanged with Clement and Johnson in the centre of midfield (if this continues we will be relegated) but Dobie came in for Horsefield up front. Less then two minutes in a cross came over and the five foot five midget Osman headed Everton into the lead. I couldn't believe it. We had only been in the bloody ground ten minutes. We began to pass it a little better and Greening continued his positive start to life at the club. On 6 mins we won a corner and Dobie nodded home to make it one - one. We went barmy, I stood on my seat and nearly fell off as it tipped up under the boinging. The rest of the half was nothing to shout about as two average sides played little football and created few chances. At half time a sizeable section of the home crowd chanted ugly songs about Rooney and his inevitable departure to Man Utd. As gut wrenching as it is to some and its happened to most teams, Everton fans can't seriously think Rooney would be better off staying with them. I mean come on, Man Utd challenge for honours every year, they have finished potless just 3 times in the last 11 years and play in the Champions League annually. Everton on the other hand have battled with relegation for much of the last decade and play in Europe on pre-season friendlies.

The second half saw the Albion perform like they have been for much of the season so far after the interval but for the Villa game - crap. How can you play so differently from one half to another? We lacked ideas going forward and had no creativity. Needless to say we failed to score. Everton played slightly better with Graveson running the show from midfield and it came as no surprise to me when they went 2 - 1 up. The goal was poor to be fair - free kick on the edge, Clement on the post then not, then back on it - you know the circus I'm on about. Ball comes in no-one marking again and he wins it for Everton. Great - first loss of the season it maybe but that's 3 points from 12. Apparently Earnshaw from Cardiff has joined for a record 3.5million - hope he brings his shooting boots with him because we bloody need it. Oh well, got to the tent at 9pm Saturday night after looking for it in the dark and went for a few jars. No game next week - what am I going to do?

Liverpool away

Now I'm sure you've heard the saying ".....you wait for one and then two come along at once.......", and the one "......things always happen in three's....."; well I'm not sure if there's one about things in fours – don't think it would be related to good fortunes anyway! Let me explain......

For the second time in a fortnight it was another familiar trip up the M6 towards the land of the Diddy Men and all things Scouse. Mr Harris had the pleasure of my Everton ticket due to Kate's Uni. friends wedding in Grimsby but I'm sure he'd have preferred to have my ticket for today's game. Anyway, Stef's turn to drive so he elected to get behind the wheel of Fay's new Clio rather than struggle with the lesser engine capacity and lack of power steering (and most things electric) in his slightly older but just as reliable P-reg. weapon. Fay's going to be chuffed driving that around all day!

Breakfast all round at Keele Services – no mushrooms or tomato for the Smiths! We rejoin the traffic heading north which is getting quite busy now. Well when both Man United and Liverpool are at home, the southern half of the country must think that there is a full scale evacuation happening – only joking! As we are cruising along, quite happily, in the middle lane, avoiding the numerous articulated lorries and coaches – Devon Reds and allsorts! We are passed, in the outside lane, by not 1, or 2, and not even 3, but 4, yes, 4 brand-spanking new silver Ford Mondeos, closely followed by a black, slightly older version. Then after only a few seconds, after we had all said how strange it is to see four identical cars one after another, a small confusion up ahead leads to a lot of brake lights and frantic braking. A red Mercedes appears at a strange angle, straddling the two outside lanes a few cars in front of us, and as we manoeuvre around him we notice a few bulbs missing and a damaged front wing – whoops! More to the point, one of the nice new shiny Mondeos is now parked up along side the central crash barrier with a nice scuff mark along the rear wing and rear bumper – double whoops! So much for a delivery of 4 new Mondeos. Now what was I saying about things in fours!

Down the M62 and towards the direction of Bootle! (There's a little mention just for you Mr Peter Jones) Stanley Park School is once again our venue for car parking and The Arckle public house seems as popular as ever. Pre- match entertainment is, as usual, courtesy of Sky Sports and just like in the George there appears to be more televisions hanging from the ceiling than people trying to watch them. However, unlike the George, each channel is showing the same game of footy so everyone can watch the same game while still talking to each other face to face. Unfortunately, some of the TV's could do with some slight adjustments. One picture looks like they're playing in Spain – bright sunshine and clear visibility, one looks like a typical autumn afternoon – slightly overcast and another looks like some footage of a game when they were still developing colour TV – various shades of grey with the odd flash of colour (Mr Chumley-Warner style from Harry Enfield).

Half two-ish, burger time! Over to the Everpool Burger van – I wonder how long it took them to come up with that name? Now if we didn't want an Everpool burger we could always have a Scouse Pie inside the ground, don't ask what's in them! Meat and veg I think, I didn't sample!

Places please gentlemen, row four thank you, just to the right of the goal. Not a bad view really, I still think the Kop doesn't look that impressive! I suppose the   all-seater side of things has taken the real character away from it. Talking of characters, which we weren't, it must be quite strange for the Liverpool and Everton fans growing up round here lately. Within a matter of weeks, Michael Owen has signed for Real Madrid to become fourth or fifth choice striker (why?) and Mr Rooney has decided to join Man United. Yeah. So what! Meggo has finally signed Rob Earnshaw from Cardiff so there! He's going to run rings round Hypia – hopefully! Well there's a shock – Earnie is on the bench. Apparently he hasn't had time to settle in properly due to International matches. Does that really matter these days, if he's good enough he'll show it, and he's got to start sometime so why not now?

The game itself starts off ok. Ref blows his whistle and then one player rolls the ball forward and then his team-mate passes it backwards to another team-mate who hoofs it forwards as his team runs forward! No seriously, the first ten or fifteen minutes seemed to pass without too much problem until Gerrard decided enough was enough and it was time for him to make his mark on the game. He played a one-two with Garcia, collected the return pass, ran across the Albion box and slotted his left foot into the bottom corner – simple really, but you know what the Albion defence is like from time to time! Clement then had a couple of chances from Koumas corners to level the scores but his headers were saved and just wide within a couple of minutes of each other. A pretty even remainder to the half but you always felt that Gerrard and Hamman could really go to town if they wanted to – remember at the Hawthorns two years ago? I don't want to talk about it – and don't ask Stef what he thought of the game, let alone the defending!

Just before the interval, Finnan's advances down the right weren't picked up quick enough by Robinson and his last ditch "rugby tackle" didn't stop him either. Into the box, round Albrechsen and another left footed shot goes into the bottom corner. I told you it was simple – why can't we stop it happening though? Two nil down at half time, surely Mr Earnshaw is going to feature soon – please? Koumas was back in the starting line up today but this first half hasn't shown us the recent form he has been in for Wales. Come on son; give a second half performance to remember – just like the one at Forest! Earnshaw makes his first appearance in a Baggies shirt shortly into the second half (no pun intended but he's not the tallest bloke). Luis Garcia responded to the strengthening of the Albion front line by firing a shot over the bar after a surging run from Cisse. Unfortunately, before Earnie had got into the action, Garcia was picked out by Gerrard (not for the first time) and he timed his run to cut inside the approaching Scimeca, evade the challenge from Purse and get a fierce shot in towards Hoult's goal. Houlty did well to parry the shot but as Garcia continued his run he reacted quicker than anyone else to fire the rebound past Hoult and into the net. Three nil and still half hour to go! If that wasn't bad enough, now it's started raining! British weather, eh! When they renovated this ground why didn't they think about making the roof cover the front rows too? Have you seen the size of the bloody roof at Newcastle? Never mind seen it….. I've touched it!

Earnshaw's first real attack saw Dudek produce a superb, reaction save to deny an instinctive debut goal after he was put through by Kanu. It appears that the only way we should play when Earnie is in the side, is to push balls through for him to run onto, after all, he is only four foot and a fag-end tall and next to Hypia it was like a Little & Large Show all over again. At one point I'm sure he was trying to get Hypia to give him a piggyback. His legs can't be tired already – he's only been on a few minutes! Two or three minutes to go and it's agreed that we shall, regrettably, make an early exit. I'm not one for a quick get away but we really didn't look like scoring today and I don't think any of us could handle seeing a fourth Liverpool goal! Back to the car and there could only have been a minute of injury time at most, we had only just crossed the main road and there was a huge cheer – but not the kind of cheer which goes with a goal celebration – I hope! We reached the car park and found that we weren't the only "early-exitters". Back down the dual carriageway, past McDonalds, onto the M62 and onto the M6. I don't think I managed the length of the M62 before I entered Z-land...... well, once you've heard the classifieds and Adrian Durham has started moaning about teams moaning about referees........you tend to........yaaawwn!.........switch off...........yaawwn!......really!

I was awoken, possibly by the lack of radio, as we were approaching the area of Stoke. No radio and an orange steering wheel-type symbol on the dash.

"What's that mean?", I queried through half open eyes,

"Dunno, son, have a look in the book!"

"Book's not in 'ere!"

"Fay's prob'ly got it at home somewhere – that's good 'ay it!"

"Its prob'ly summet to do with the power steering. You won't be able to tell on the motorway though."

We pull into the next services, fortunately only a few miles down the motorway, as Stef is telling us how this is the third time now that the car has had an electrical fault on it. Yes, it is power steering – that symbol – because Stef now knows what it must be like to drive a double-decker bus around a layout of small cones! Mind you, as you will recall, his Clio is the one without all of the electrical luxuries of the modern models! We park up and try restarting the engine – dead as a proverbial dodo!

Stef rings Fay – she's definitely not chuffed. Smithy rings the RAC – he might be covered in someone else's car. Fay tells Stef her AA policy details etc and we give the "fourth" emergency service a ring! "He'll be with you within the hour sir; he has your mobile number to contact you."

Smithy tells the RAC thanks, but no thanks! We all go inside for some refreshments and sustenance. Who said you should always have a blanket and some chocolate in case of an emergency? Or you could just use the facilities at a service station! Even though they are extortionate prices, we sit down and have tea/coffee and biscuits – how civilised – while we wait for the AA.

After half an hour or so, we have contact from friendly AA man Bob. He does the usual, tries starting different ways, checks this, checks that, explains this, baffles us with that – look Bob mate, can u get it sorted or what? Well to cut a long story short, it was a loose connection between the starter motor, alternator, and battery. Basically, the battery wasn't being charged as we were driving and hence, things slowly started going! Personally I think it's a bit harsh that the radio is the first to go, but I suppose safety first and all that! I know it's not essential to the workings of a car but you've got to have some music on haven't you?

We finally arrive back home about 9o'clock rather than about half seven, but it's been an eventful day all round! Still time to meet the girls in the Wernley to sink a few jars and amaze them with our newly acquired car knowledge!

Fulham home

5 games into the new season and already some managers have been sacked. But not Megson, after all he has got us to the play-offs and had two promotions and a season in the Premiership in five years of stewardship. Well you would like to think so wouldn't you? The media has been alive with speculation that Megson and Peace have fallen out and it's only a matter of time for Mego. I've heard all the stories about Megson being a first division manager and that he has taken us as far as he can but this is ridiculous surely. Who will we replace him with? Why has the Board let him spend the most money we have ever had? What has he actually done wrong? Okay, he keeps playing Robinson at left back and Johnson in midfield, he never plays Sakiri and is playing our left back in centre midfield and signs players without playing them - Gera and Contra but apart from that ..... Oh well he was still in charge for today's game with the mighty Fulham.

Now Rodney Marsh is not exactly everyone's best mate down the Albion and once again this morning he slagged us off in his usual over the top, "I'm trying to be controversial because I'm brainless" way.

Basically he said straight out as bold as you like .."West Brom are not a Premiership team, on or off the field". Jeff Stelling replied by pointing out we have a history and were always viewed as a top-flight club, to which the washed up Cockney quipped "Yeah, a thousand years ago", then he laughed. There was a time I would have spat at the TV but now I just feel pity for the idiot because his whole existence on the panel is based on off the cuff mindless remarks in the hope that some fans will get riled and so improve viewing figures. What he says has no substance whatsoever and each week he is simply used like a freak show in the circus. He achieved very little in the game and played for 3 of the countries top clubs - Fulham, Man City and QPR!!! Stick to back street stand up Rodney and give everyone a break.

I managed a quick one in the Wern before the game. Just before kick off I peered across to the away section and saw the front half of the allocation empty, leaving about 500 fans at best. Pathetic. Fulham's following was on a par with Watford, Gillingham and Crewe from last year I'm not joking, but I suppose they're a Premiership club aren't they Rodders? Now last week they were dealt some hideous refereeing decisions by Halsey as he single-handedly ensured Arsenal maintained their unbeaten run by bowing to player intimidation. No question at all then that Fulham were going to adopt the same approach today if anything went against them and so it proved. We battered them first half with Van Der Saar making two top class saves then hand ball in the area gifted us a penalty. One nil surely, that's the least we deserved. Now I reckon it was about 5 minutes from the ref. awarding a pen to the moment we took it. Why? Because the Fulham players hounded the referee in such a way he was forced back towards the touchline. It was so obvious they had "learnt" from their experience last week with Arsenal but to me it was disgusting. Fair play to the ref. he booked one of the protesters - should have booked the lot. Anyway, Van Der Saar then tried a bit of gamesmanship, which is basically football talk for down right bloody cheating by approaching the penalty spot and checking the ball is on it just as the player is about to take his shot. He then walks back towards his goal, stops at least 3 yards from the line, turns and stares at the floor like he's dropped something. £3million pound man Earnshaw runs up and I'm thinking what are you doing? Their keeper isn't in goal so he can't let you take it yet… can he? Blasts it over the bar and the ref. runs off - play on, goal kick. There was no way he was going to ask us to take it again and incur the wrath of the Fulham players again was he? Tossers. How we went in 0 - 0 at half time I'll never know (we failed to take our chances).

Second half and I got that horrible feeling you get when you've played really well but haven't scored and just know the opposition will if they get a chance. Fulham played better after the break but still didn't impress me one bit. They moaned about everything and time wasted like the foreigners they are. Dioup or something then got wound up by Purse and lashed out at him - goodbye. 10 men - surely this is our time. On about 70 mins they broke down the right and waltzed past two Albion defenders. The cross was low and the finish from Cole true. I should be well used to this now but the feeling you get when the Albion do this to you never changes. Their minibus load of supporters jumped around and laughed at us while I clock watched. With about ten to go Boa Morte broke free and ran across Clement who clipped his heels so was sent packing, but something must have been said because a good old fashioned melee ensued. Then right in the middle of it all Andy Cole punched Clement full blown with a big haymaker. I couldn't believe it, what a dick - goodbye to you too. They were down to nine now. Surely we could get something, if Fulham won this game it would have been a real injustice. With 2 mins to go Koumas swung a corner over and Kanu stooped to head home. 1 - 1 it finished. To be fair the ref. did all he could but we should have beat a poor Fulham side today. Still no win this season and revitalised Newcastle away next week!!

Newcastle away

You just would not believe how far Newcastle is from my house. It took us about 4 hours to reach the Tyne then another hour to park the car – nice. Last night we all went to see Tony Palmer the comedian at the Dudley Village. Now, our connection with Tony goes way back in fact, 16 years to be precise. Let me explain, when we were about 14 one of our older mates had a tape of this Black Country comedian who we had never heard of but he had us in stitches for hours. The tape was re-run on battered old tape recorders for the next 10 years and his one liners became part of our everyday vocabulary. I built up a picture of what this comedian would look like and to be honest I thought he was probably dead considering his jokes on the tape referred to last year and the Falklands crisis!! When he came on I just heard him speaking and it had me doubled up, he hadn't changed his act really or his accent luckily in all this time. Not sure the political correct brigade of the 21st century would laugh much but as Tone himself would say .. f**k 'em.

By the time we reached Scotch Corner I was ready to come home. How do the Geordies follow their team all over the country from there? I suppose they have been born into that national remoteness and have a different feel for distance than us Midlanders, I mean, 2 hours down the M5 and we're not going any further, hence the development of Weston Super Mare!! It's the great North run this weekend – it was the last time we came funnily enough so traffic into Geordieland was savage. We finally parked on some Quick Fit or something 5 mins from the ground. We went to the Labour Club and met that doorman last time if you remember and tasted "peas puddin'", but this year we felt it was a bit late so headed for the ground early. After the ten flights of concrete stairs we had a beer and some oxygen. Our seats were on row X this time, one from the back – nice. St James' Park is very impressive but you are so far up in the away section it is ridiculous. If you go in a straight line east from Newcastle you first come to Denmark before anywhere else and I'm sure I could see Hans Christian Anderson at one point when we had a corner in the second half. Earnshaw, Albion's record signing and centre forward was 80 – 1 to score first in a 1 – 0 win. Read into that what you like but it's not the best thing to inspire you. By the way, a Newcastle win of 6 – 0 was the same odds as 2 – 1 Albion – nice.

For an hour there was no difference between the sides I swear then Purse was red carded for his second booking – good bye. He trudged off and went down the tunnel accompanied by our chances of getting anything from the game. By now Megson had taken our 3.5 million-pound goal scorer off at half time for tactical reasons, best known to himself and swapped the creative midfielder Koumas for Gera. Not sure what he was hoping for but we were 3 down in ten minutes soon after. I was gutted as we sloped off back to the car, missing Horsefield's consolation in the process. Smithy drove 400 miles on Saturday and all me, Gav and Paul did was eat, drink and sit – very healthy I heard. I can't believe we are in such a mess, yet our squad is much better than two years ago. God knows what Megson and Peace are doing, the press are having a laugh while the majority of fans are scratching their heads in total bewilderment – I know I am. I reckon the next 3 games will have a big bearing on our season and Meggo's fate. Bolton at home, Norwich at home and Palace away. If we lose them there's no way back for the manager in my opinion. Can't believe I'm saying that after 7 games but such is football.

The drive home consisted of semi conscious sleeping, sweets, belching and farting – you know the usual stuff. I just couldn't help thinking the season might even be over now and if not over then a boring struggle ahead. Surely I'm not losing interest with my beloved? I'm beginning to think maybe a change is what we need but Sir Bobby Robson? Not sure about him, he past retirement age fifty years ago didn't he? Oh well, we made the Wernley for about half nine to have a few beers and try and forget our 13 hour ordeal. Football is funny isn't it? I wonder how many thousands of fans gave up the whole of Saturday to football. Talk about it, get angry, upset, elated, drunk, etc. People all over the world live and die football and yet sometimes I stop and think, "they're only kicking a ball about" but then soon after I'm consumed with the irrepressible force that has you in its grip. I still get the 'hairs standing up' feeling when I clap the Baggies out and when I think back to the emotion I felt as a boy when I scored for the school it never ceases to amaze me. Laugh if you want but I still dream of scoring for the Albion and Cryille Regis could get me to do anything (easy, not that).

I'm reading Gazza's book at the moment and am getting more and more astonished with each page. People have said that you simply cannot help but feel pulled towards Gazza once you've spent some time with him. Reading his brutally honest account of an amazing life makes me feel pretty much the same. It has made me want to meet him or write to him to maybe just say don't worry things will be okay and I don't even know him! He was a truly outstanding player and his life story even more so. He links much of his emotions to his experiences of death – friends, family, etc. times when he can't handle it. This makes me think of my Nan who died a couple of weeks ago, she was an amazing lady who taught me a lot and around the same time, a bloke who used to play football with us on a Sunday morning in the gym. I didn't know him long, he just came along, played in goal in his scruffy kit, had a roll up at the end then drove off in various bangers each week. Apparently he took his own life with some sort of firearm because he couldn't handle it anymore. His name was Guy and he was alright.

Bolton home

Now for today's game, Fay has kindly donated her ticket to Dad (Graham) so that he can sit with us in the Smethwick to watch his beloved Bolton play at the Hawthorns. I'm not sure if you are aware but Vernon Kay is from Bolton! You can tell this not only from his accent, but due to the fact that he mentions this fact every few seconds on Radio One and on T4. It's as if his name has been changed to Vernon Kay-from-Bolton. Anyway, where was I? Yes, Dad's always been a big fan of Sam Allerdyce's and loves to watch the northern Wanderers whenever he can. He's been to all the Cup Finals and everything. Scarves, mugs, hats, badges, you name it he's got it! His most treasured possession is a scale model of the Reebok Stadium which he created out of used matches. It really is a work of art!

No seriously, you've probably guessed – I'm joking! Fay is out with the Anchor Boys from 5th West Bromwich Company today at some farm-type place somewhere down by Warwick. Kate has also gone with her to help supervise the lads but she should be back in time for the match! Fay's got to stay at the church because they're having a sleep-over too. That means, however, today's game should be an interesting one with a few goals and Albion will probably win. If this was a few years ago I would also add that Bob Taylor will score too. This always seemed to be the outcome whenever Fay missed a game on previous occasions. So fingers crossed and all that! After meeting the Smith twins at the George, Shepherd's Taxis arrive on cue to ferry us to the game.

Pre-match comments from Tom Ross reveal that Horsefield and Kanu are the preferred choice up front for today's game. No Earnshaw in the starting eleven but he cost us £3,000,000! Ok, fair enough, that changes the scorers but there is a distinct feeling around the turnstiles that we could get something from this game. I think it's time for a bet don't you? Stef opts for Koumas to score first and Albion to win 2-1 for £2. Sounds good – I'll have a quid on that too, and I'll have Kanu to score first and Albion to win 3-1..... £2 on that, and I'll also have a straight bet for Albion to win 3-0…..yeh £2 on that too. You never know with the Albion! If Earnie not starting was bad enough, we now hear that Koumas hasn't made the starting line up either – and he hasn't even made the bench! Stef hurries back down to change his bet; I can't be bothered (typical!) as I've got my other two still. As the teams emerge it looks like Johnson and Scimeca are our midfield maestros for today.

After a sluggish start and some early Bolton pressure, the Baggies managed to peg back the visitors with some exciting and attacking football which on another afternoon, well evening actually, would have resulted in a couple of goals. (Forgot to mention that this game has been selected for Sky Television which means games can be played at which ever silly hour the hierarchy of the modern game decide. Not sure who came up with 5.15pm on a Saturday but anyway.)

Unfortunately, Gera's long range effort only managed the side netting; Horse could only hit his shot straight at Jaaskelainen; Gera was certainly making the most of his start with another shot which was deflected over and a rebound acrobatically going wide. All this after Big Dave had caused panic with a bullet header from a corner. Now just remember that Bolton are flying high at present in something like fourth place behind Everton of all people! Bolton's aging striker Les Ferdinand should really have had one eye on the ball and one eye on the goal half way through the first half because as a Bolton corner came into the Albion area, he somehow managed to volley the ball away from the Baggies goal – cheers Les! Bolton did hit the woodwork before the break but it really was all Albion, possibly due to the fact that mid-way through the half, Jay-jay Ockocha had to be replaced to the relief of the Hawthorns faithful. Not only this, but the amount of chances we created meant that we should have gone in at least a goal to the good. Horsefield and Gera were again the main threats on the Bolton goal. After the restart, more pressure from Albion. This time Gera's low cross from the right was met by Kanu who gracefully slotted the ball into the back of the net from close range. Shortly afterwards, Gera's efforts paid off as he extended Albion's lead with a well timed run to the front post where he met Greening's corner with an unchallenged header. Boing Boing – well this guy doesn't need springs or a trampoline – backwards cartwheels and summersaults. 5.9 from the Hungarian judge. Apparently it would have been 6.0 but his feet were apart when he landed!

Right, that's 2-0. All bet's still on! Just one more goal now lads and then you can let one in if you like – I don't mind. £300 quid if you do! Stef would like a consolation goal in the 92 minute for Bolton if that's ok guys? It is only £102 though.

They nearly did get a goal from a 25-yard curler, which kept Hoult on his toes and then a killer blow! Big Sam decides to send on some Greek bloke who had a good game in Portugal in the summer or something! He takes a free kick from out wide on the left which somehow manages to float across the box without a single touch from anyone. You've guessed it, a quick bounce on the hallowed turf and straight into the back of the net. Come on lads, you've got to either hold on for another 15 minutes or so, or get your arses up the other end and score another.

Now you must have been in a similar situation where you're willing the ref to blow his whistle, when you've chewed off all your nails, you're sitting so far forward on your seat that the bloke in front thinks he's giving you a piggy back, you're gripping your betting slip so tight that the carbon copy has nearly rubbed off, and then all of a sudden; almost as if your beating Man United at home in the Champion's League Final and instead of checking his watch, the ref asks Mr Ferguson how long he would like for injury time; up goes the board from the fourth official – 4 minutes! What the......!

Finally, at last, the waiting is over, we've done it! A Premiership win...... and Stef won a bet at the Albion! But as I said before we should have expected it really, Fay wasn't here to see it – she has got £100 to spend on shopping though!

Norwich Home

I don't care what Tom Ross says Norwich at home is a game you win if you have any aspirations of staying in the division. Nevermind all this BS about there's no easy game at this level, you get nothing for free, etc. etc - if we have made any progress this year after spending more money than I can remember then we will push Norwich aside. This is not the Albion of two years ago when we bought nobody and played with our hearts on our sleeves with starry eyes expecting and getting nothing.

Well, it shouldn't be, not after our experience of two years and a far stronger squad of players. That is the bottom line - we should have moved on and up now, I'm not talking about Europe or anything daft like that I'm just saying we should now be challenging the likes of Bolton, Southampton, etc. for the right to finish above the likes of Palace and Norwich. I truly believe that. It's for this reason I approached this game expecting, yes expecting just like a Blue Nose would to win. Norwich won the old first division last year ahead of us and added a free Swede to their squad in the summer. We spent the best part of 10million quid and a manager worth his salt should reap some sort of reward from that outlay.

After helping the Queen shift some stuff to Nans me and Vince met Gav and the Smiths at the George for a beer. Burg told me Sully had 21 pints last night so I'm going to ring Noris Mcwirter later to see if that's some kind of record or something. Anyway, we made our seats just in time for the kick off. Fair play to Norwich they filled their allocation and made some noise but so they should - we did two years ago in excitement. Team announced - £3million Earnshaw (who scored in a World Cup qualifier against Poland in the week) along with £2.5million Koumas who also played for Wales in the same game on the bench. So Megson truly believes in his heart and head I suppose that we can afford to not play these two players and that First Division stalwart Horsefield and "run around town" Johnson will give us a better option. Okay, stick with it, it is the team that beat Bolton so fair dos. Usually I try to discuss the game at this point but I genuinely think there is nothing to say. We huffed and puffed, they hit it long to Huckerby and crossed their fingers and so it went on. Moore won at least 8 flick ons in their box but the nearest player each time was on the edge of the area probably concerned with tracking back or doing their 7 miles aye Megson? The Albion were crying out for pace up front but our pocket rocket was kept on the bench. Gera and Greening tried their best to create something and Kanu worked to produce an opening but there was nothing there. We needed a change big time. On the hour Earnshaw finally stood on the side ready to come on - it's only half-hour but him and Kanu should be good. Number held up and I rub my eyes, surely not, he's not bringing off Kanu and leaving the ineffective Horse on? Jesus Megson what are you doing?

Still nothing to shout about, there's nothing created, the singing has stopped and to be honest Norwich who give the title Workmanlike a new meaning are playing the better football and look like snatching it. Sub number 2 warmed up now - the most creative player at the club, Koumas comes on for Johnson surely so we can have as much flair as possible to go for the 3 points. But no, Megson decides to bring off our most consistent midfielder Greening instead. Still no improvement and Koumas swans around with the body language of a pissed off teenager - disgusting I know but who is his man-manager? Who has sucked the creativity out of him? Who dropped him completely from the squad because he was unhappy at being subbed? Who shouts at him constantly from start to finish? We are not a club that can afford to destroy players of quality because we're not happy with them. Is there not an alternative way of getting the best out of a player other than punishment? Little old-fashioned if you ask me. Anyway back to the 0 - 0 thrilling spectacle against Norwich. Last 15 and one goal will surely win this, Norwich make a change, forward for forward and press for the winner. We still don't appear to be at the races then Megson produces a move that can only be described as legendary all for the wrong reasons. He brings Gera off who is an attacking right winger and replaces him with Robinson who is an average First Division left back. Now for some of you that means nothing so I'll put it into some kind of universal perspective. Man Utd are at home going in to the last 10 minutes looking to win the game. Then Fergie takes Ronaldo off and replaces him with Phil Neville - enough said. Reading this you probably think I'm a Megson hater but as I've said before that is not the case. I just cannot agree with any of his substitutions today or his starting 11, judging by the thousands of fans around me I wasn't the only one. The final whistle went, 0 - 0 and for the first time in a very long time a sizeable section booed. I had to agree. I wasn't booing the players, I just wanted Megson to realise that the people who were paying his wages were not happy one bit with a performance like that and he for one had to take some of the blame as he picked the side and trained/motivated them and made the decisions. As I write this I am convinced Norwich will be relegated so a whimpering performance like that tells me a lot.

We drove home so annoyed it was untrue then to top it all we had to listen to Tom brown nose Ross come out with more excuses for the team than a Labour MP. They were tired, they had been travelling, yawn,

yawn. He even said he would prefer a runner in his team than a half-hearted kid and I know what his point is but we are not Birchfield Harriers Tom. Johnson meets Megson's standards of 7 miles a game but I could do that. He does nothing with the ball and that is the name of the game, full stop end of story. We go to Palace next week in another game that we should win. They crept through the play offs last year and have spent less than two rupees on strengthening their squad - watch this space for the negative team selection. Oh well it's only a game and Norwich enjoyed themselves I suppose.

Crystal Palace away

Please tell me Megson didn't honestly treat the players the way it was reported this week. Apparently, he trained them on Monday and wasn't happy so when he still wasn't happy on Tuesday he called training off after half an hour and sent everyone home with the instructions to return on Thursday! What the hell is going on? What did they do wrong? Weren't they running far enough? Didn't they look as if they were trying hard enough, after all that's all that matters doesn't it? Palace started bottom and reminded me of us two years ago - hard-working but nothing else. They had the little blue nose AJ scoring goals but nothing more to trouble anyone. It's early days but I'll say it now - Palace will be relegated. This was a game we had to be positive in, it was a game we could easily win like the rest of the teams in the Premiership. I heard the team and most of my fears were correct - a defensive 3-5-2 with Robinson back in from nowhere, still no Contra, Greening subbed and Koumas has a mysterious back complaint! This is becoming a joke.

So where do you want me to start?

The weather?

The journey?

The match?

The ground?

Well, let's start at the very beginning. Apparently, it's a very good place to start!

The journey itself started for me at about 08:30, short burst up the M5/M6 to Scott Arms to hand over the works call phone to Tom, an engineer from work who's covering call out for me during today. Kate has kindly agreed to the use of her car for my share of the driving so it's a debut journey for the Toyota Yaris. The first pick-up is Elm Croft at 09:40 and then round the corner to the Smith household in Tame Rise. There's also a new direction of travel today as we venture down the M40 towards "the big smoke". Usual stop for fried provisions at Cherwell Valley and to our horror, the Albion coaches have beaten us to it – Albion everywhere!

Now anyone who has travelled to London by car will tell you that to get to the M25 will take between an hour and an hour and a half. According to the map, this may also be the majority of the journey, but to get anywhere around or inside the M25 will take you another hour, hour and a half, two, three hours just be prepared to sit in your car at some point along your journey around the London Orbital Route. Our journey took us past the ever-expanding Heathrow Airport, where it looks like Terminal 5 is well underway; a mass of road works surrounded by huge piles of earth, concrete pillars and men in day glow jackets doing... well... not much! Variable speed limits should allow easy flow of traffic but instead of the highlighted 50 and 40 speed restrictions we were stuck at the more realistic speed of 0 mph!

Off at junction 7 and up towards Croydon, more traffic, more road works, more sitting and waiting; and now its started to rain! I'll come onto that in a moment. A slight diversion from the Internet away-guide directions but we're soon back on track, and probably further up the queue of traffic – which was nice! If it wasn't bad enough that it's started to rain, the footy has already started! No, not the Albion; the early game on Sky! We're normally in the pub, supping on a few beers and watching the game before the rush when the coaches arrive. Not today, we've only just got past Croydon. After noticing Adrian Chiles (Baggies fan from Radio Five and Match of the Day 2) and his mate walking to the ground, we finally arrive in the area of Selhurst Park four hours after setting off! Iceland being the preferred choice of parking (just outside Reykjavik), we park, pay and display, and at long last head for the pub – Wetherspoons. Fantastic – bottles of Corona £0.99 and we get to see most of the second half of the televised game.

I must warn you that the last sentence of the previous paragraph is as good as it gets for a while, so if you're feeling a bit down at the moment or you're not up to the odd bit of bad language, can I suggest you skip to the next game and come back to these next few pages at a later date! Are we sitting comfortably?

Then I'll begin…

We had met up with Jonah (Wayne Jones) in the pub and he was giving us his usual guided tour of London type monologue as we walked to the ground. We spotted a house on the corner which to say the least, needed some work doing to it! Without thinking of the inevitable Jonah-style answer, we questioned Mr Jones as to how much the property would be worth? Now bearing in mind he moved to London with a 7 million pound bonus (not really – but it was a ridiculous amount), we should have guessed his reply would be met with some disagreement!

"Well, put it like this Stef, even I couldn't afford it!"

"Why not…… how much is it then?"

"Probably go for about 400 grand!"

Now this house is literally down the road from the Palace ground, large semi-detached with three, maybe four bedrooms, most windows looked rotten, needed painting and had a large front garden all over grown… I think you can guess the language in our responses!

As we approach the ground, which has a Sainsbury's built into the one end of it, we are bombarded by people giving out free Pepperami sticks, new hot flavour or something, so us, gullible Midlanders accept the freebies and tuck in! Did I say they were a new hot flavour? Sorry I should have said an extremely hot, burn the back of your bastard throat flavour! Don't think I'll be eating anymore of that, thank you very much! So in through ancient turnstiles and next stop toilets, those Corona's are passing through already. Toilets, toilets, any signs for toilets? No, just a line of fucking port-a-loos. A Premiership ground with port-a-loos, what the fuck is going on? Ok so we've done the necessaries, now for some food.

"Hot dog son?"

"Yeah. Rapid"

"E'are….. pay her when she gives 'em you. I need a piss now!"

Ten minutes later and we finally get our food. Not sure exactly what the problem was, no queue, just some half-soaked cockney-Jamaican attitude! This delay means that by the time we have found our seats (or seat at first – Stef thought his seat was knackered until he realised it was still in the upright position!) the game has kicked off and………. I'll just mention the shitty wooden seats with no legroom, hardly any light to see what or indeed who you might be sitting on and iron girders blocking the view every so often. I suppose they are doing a good job in holding the roof up though – build a new stand – please!

So where was I, oh yes, the game! The game has already kicked off and would you Adam-and-eve it some bloke crosses a ball into the Albion box and Hall is left totally unmarked at the back post where he is able to direct his header across Hoult's goal and into the back of the net – one nil down and I haven't even finished my hot dog! From Albion's next corner, Darren Moore somehow manages to direct a free-header down towards goal but with such power that it bounces up and over the bar with the keeper helpless. And to make matters worse, Palace's next break sees Gaardsoe slip, a cross from the left, Albrechtsen managed to nudge Johnson with a little bit too much force and the ref. blows for a penalty! Johnson, two nil!

Now the last few games have seen a change in the fans appreciation of Lord Mego. Gone are the days where he could do nothing wrong, well, perhaps he can still do no wrong in some fans eyes. In my opinion, his team selections and substitutions of the last few games have seemed a little if not rather strange. How Andy Johnson can start every match when all he seems to do is chase shadows in the middle of the park is strange enough as it is. Now I know I said before that Johnson is the nearly man of the Albion, but just lately he seems to be running round much more than usual and doing not a lot else! I remember Tom Ross saying, when we signed him from Forest, "He's a proper ball winner. He'll tackle a barn door if you asked him too", I might suggest the Albion dish-out some barn doors for the visiting team to carry round next match if it will help! Don't get me wrong, he's not a shit player, he's just not good enough for this level of football I don't think – give him a few games off will you please? So far this season, after signing them on deadline day, we still haven't seen anything of this Contra bloke who's got 50-odd caps for Romania so surely he's worth a run in the side; and Earnshaw has had about 20 minutes in two games to show his worth! Come on Megson, stop being so stubborn, have a change round will you? Why he keeps leaving Koumas out of the starting eleven and subbing Gera during a game is beyond me and don't let me start on about the disappearance of Sakiri............

Today was another strange selection, we've played 4-4-2 during the last few games and it's seemed to work ok, today it appears he's gone for a 3-5-2. No Koumas at all and Greening starting on the bench alongside Inamoto! Well, anyway, Greening comes on for Albrechtsen and we change back to a 4-4-2 formation. Shortly after the second goal goes in, Paul Smith expresses his feelings on the game by announcing that he wished he had stayed in the pub and watch the game on Sky instead! With not that much improvement even with Greening being more effective on the pitch rather than on the bench, Paul decides that half an hour is all he needs to see and makes his way back to the Wetherspoons!

Half way through the second half the game was almost back on and then over in the space of a few seconds. A surging run from Robinson ends with a pass across the box to Earnshaw who controls, turns, and fires a shot against the bar. Straight away Palace break and after crossing the half-way line and closing in on the Baggies goal, Johnson strikes from the edge of the box across the rain-soaked grass and into Hoult's net off the foot of the post. Three – nil. Cue departure of Andy Smith who has definitely seen enough now! I think me and Stef managed to hold out for about another ten before deciding that if the journey back home is anything like the one on the way down, we'd be better off starting back than watching this pile of shite in blue and white stripes!

The weather conditions haven't helped at all really today, shitty drizzle "…it's that fine rain…" on the way down and on the way to the match. Rained all game – still, no excuse for performance, they should be used to this shit weather by now; and by the time we came out the ground it's now pissing it down! So we're soaked before we get back to the car and we've got at least three hours before we get back home – great! Kate's car completes the return journey in one piece after a stop at the services for refuelling and the now familiar coffees/teas and fruit shortcakes and cookies. It's still raining by the way. After discussing just how bad the team performed today and the forthcoming away fixtures, Andy decides that he's not going to another away game while Megson's still in charge! I don't think he needs to go that far but I can see where he's coming from.

Now I wonder if there was anyone listening to our conversation at the services who may have had some bearing in the Albion hierarchy?

That was about half past seven on Saturday evening and by Tuesday afternoon Gary Megson had been "relieved of his managerial duties" at the club! Apparently he's been put on "Gardening Duties" or some bull-shit phrase meaning he hasn't been sacked but he isn't in charge at the Albion anymore!!

Chelsea home

Chelsea annoy me probably more than any other club (local rivals not included obviously). This is not based on hate, or incidents involving the Albion etc. it is simply to do with everything that Chelsea stands for. Rodney Trotter supports Chelsea for the same reason Wolfie Smith supports Fulham - we are meant to feel sorry for them. These TV story lines are not that long ago and yet today Chelsea are portrayed as a massive club without doubt. This is not the reason for my dislike, however, the reason I have no affection for them is based on listening to footy phone-ins and the media in general. Chelsea have used, and this is a conservative estimate, about 150 players I reckon in the last 3 years. They have spent a hideous amount of money on hoards of foreign players. This money has come from the late Mr Harding and now a Russian "business" man who has "always had an affection for Chelsea FC". Their whole existence is in the hands of someone who is so detached from their history and from genuine football itself it's ridiculous and yet we still have the Cockney twang on the radio chirping on about how great Chelsea are and they're gonna do this and that. "We're part of the big 3" - don't make me laugh. Chelsea FC are not fit to lick the boots of Arsenal in terms of stature let alone Man Utd and I haven't even mentioned Liverpool. You see my annoyance lies right there - they talk as if they've been around for years, always up there challenging through history but the simple fact is they haven't and their current success is based on foreign cash and superficial heroes. We sang "where were you when you were shit?" and that's my point. For me Chelsea have no soul, the real fans like Rodney Trotter are long gone.

The Albion are post Gary Megson. Statistics often amaze me but when I realised GM was the longest serving manager since the War or something like that I was dumbfounded. When you add the fact that he gained promotion back to the top flight twice when around 14 others failed once, it sounds strange to think he is no longer with us, and no he didn't leave to get a better job! Trouble was, he didn't get on with the Chairman, he fell out with key players, he seemed too concerned with not losing rather than trying to win and again, he didn't get on with the Chairman. Frank Emmerdale Farm Burrows took the reigns for the visit of Chelsea, flat cap and all. The first half was good for us because basically they never found their rhythm. We hassled and hurried and knocked at the door but it somehow wouldn't open and I kind of knew what was coming next. In first half injury time we decided to not bother marking at a corner, so Terry headed freely towards goal and Gallas diverted it away from Hoult to make it 1 - 0. The Ref. blew after the first touch of the ball from the centre. Nice. I just knew we wouldn't stage a remarkable second half come back so simply sat there resigned to my fate.

The second half proved to be as I guessed it would. Chelsea, but for a 5-min spell battered us into submission and ran out 4 - 1 winners. We had no idea and were totally outplayed by a superior side. The new manager has to look at the centre of midfield. I'd be gutted with Johnson and Clement or Johnson and Scimeca in Div 1 to be honest. AJ is a poor water carrier as Cantona would say and Clemmo is our bloody left back! The most creative midfielder we have is on the bench. Gera scored another screamer but it mattered not as they say. Chelsea sang "we are top of the league" as Southampton were beating Arsenal at Highbury in injury time. Then Danny Boy had a call from his dad saying that The Arse had scored and he went mad, (H's fella you see, from the capital - a Gooner in the Albion end). "Get in there you fackin' beauty, cam on, have that" and so he went on. Luckily, the Smethwick End had emptied enough to not really notice this Cockney givin it big - thank God! Names have been mentioned to replace Mego - Strachan, Hoddle, Robson (both Bs), etc. but one sent a shiver down my spine - John Gregory. Am I the only bloke who frowns every time I see or hear this man on Sky TV? I mean lets look at his record shall we - spent more money at Villa than any other manager in their history and won nothing. Signed a player from the former Eastern Bloc for £6million, never played him then let him go for nothing. He came out with quotes like the shooting of Dwight Yorke, (for wanting to leave a trophy-less second rate team like Villa for European Cup honours at Man Utd) that made me cringe. He then went on to "manage" or mismanage, as it should be Derby County to the point of financial ruin where players weren't being paid but he still wanted his contract money long after he had gone when Derby were unable to pay for a meat pie. He sits on the panel of "experts" and has the audacity to give his opinion, when the decent thing to do would be to apologise for destroying much of what he has touched and then to go away quietly. Please God not him. We've got the Saints away next week who are also going through a sticky patch (that's football talk for shit), so it should be a great game!

Southampton away

Put oil in Fay's car, blew up the tyres, filled up with petrol and it wasn't even 9am - have that! Yesterday my knee decided to start giving me some serious gip. I hadn't knocked it or anything like that but basically I couldn't get up the stairs last night without dragging my left leg behind me like a dead weight. That reminds me I saw Wardy last week. He was telling me about his son and how chuffed he was and everything but was a little concerned about who the father was, as he was only using his right foot and was crap with his left! Does anyone remember Wardy's first job as a gas fitter in Foley House? I know it was a big thing but I wasn't expecting all those people watching on Tame hill and who invited Central News? Anyway, my knee was vibing but I could still drive funnily enough. We reached Southampton in good time for a beer. There was no room on the Hotel carpark (Sorry Malc) so we found a little pay and display a bit further round. We had a beer in the King Alfred or something but upstairs made the Holiday Inn Beirut seem like 5 star so we left. Malc pointed us in the direction of Le Tissiers feet, which we found after I hobbled like an 80-year-old cripple to which I received the customary sympathy - stop complaining you dickhead, etc. and your left foot was crap anyway. We had a few in there then headed for the ground.

St Mary's is The Riverside, is most new grounds in the last ten years to be honest. The Albion played in all white to avoid a clash, which was a surprise. Jack Sugden left Koumas on the bench again and stuck with our runners in Midfield but apart from that we looked okay. The game started poorly to be honest with neither side seemingly capable of playing any decent football. Then after about half an hour we lost possession on the edge of the box, the ball was swung back in far post and one of their forwards ghosted in totally free to head down into the bottom corner, 1 - 0. I had to watch my language because out of the 3200 seats we sold (Blues took about 1500 last week) mine ended up next to a pupil from school and his mom! We began to play it a little neater and more importantly, more direct towards the end of the first half, when the ball was knocked in and Greening headed goalwards for Earnshaw to tap past their keeper for 1 - 1. We went barmy. I stood on my chair and cupped both ears at this bloke in the home section as if to say I can't hear anything now mate, sad I know but in that split second you lose control of yourself, I swear you really do. Few minutes later I was at it again, bad knee and all. The ball was bobbling around on the edge of the Saints area and it sat up nicely for Earnshaw to volley into the turf. It bounced wickedly as it flew into the net for 2 - 1. You beauty, get in there. Half time came and we looked good for the lead, I couldn't believe it.

The second half started with a golden chance for the Baggies to put the game beyond the Saints. A mix up in their 6-year box saw the keeper fumble and be grounded and their centre half sliced a clearance that had me shouting banana foot loudly. The ball went up in the air and fell perfectly for Earnshaw 4 yards out. He tried an overhead kick that was the right thing to do to be honest, not a Brazilian type effort because it didn't need to be, just a sort of half-hook, half flick type shot that flashed wide when he really should have scored. That would have been 3 - 1 game over I'm sure, even for the Harry. The rest of the half was shite. The bloke in front did his best to annoy the steward, you know the usual thing - "sit down mate please", "tell them to sit down" (he motions towards the home fans), "sorry mate this is my area, just sit down please mate" "why, I've paid me money", etc. etc. He sits down, then proceeds to ask another steward what his problem was and told him to stop looking at him. Then I thought it was gonna go off as the steward told him the section was non-smoking and he would have to put the fag out. "Where's the signs?" etc. he went on. I was thinking "mate just shut up and watch the match". I looked at my watch, there were 3 minutes to go. Albion actually looked comfortable against a very poor Saints side but you still can't trust the Albion I'm telling you. I've learnt that over the years if nothing else! They broke down the right and whipped in a cross-shot, Robinson stuck out a leg and the ball rocketed off his boot past

Hoult into the net 2 - 2. I was devastated. The last couple of minutes plus injury time were awful, we nearly lost it! A point against Southampton away you might see as good but when your winning 2 - 1 with no time left its like you've lost. Plus when you look at the bigger picture, we've missed a great opportunity to bury them because they are really in the mire at the moment and still have golden boy Beattie out.

I hobbled back to the car like a war veteran and we headed home. Tea and biscuits on the services is becoming a nice little ritual of late but it doesn't hide the worry that we face in the coming weeks. We've no manager, creativity in midfield or the players to really change it. Our next 3 games are Boro, Arsenal and Man Utd. I don't think Jesus himself would get the Albion through them unscathed and then what? Bottom of the league and looking at Division 1, seriously it's that bad. The January window needs to be open early and we need to buy at least 2 players. The centre of midfield needs strengthening big time and we need another forward, full back and centre half, apart from that we're the best team you'll ever see.

Boro' home

So here we are then, the dawning of a new era! Move over Megson, F*** off Frank (sorry that's a bit strong but I couldn't think of anything else – you did ok really but I think we'll see a few changes off the pitch now), it's time for the return of Captain Marvel. Arise Sir Bryan!

Some people wanted his older namesake and some people definitely didn't want him, but I think Bryan Robson could be the man to turn the season around. He's definitely a big enough name in the game and he did reasonably well at Boro before a rather disappointing spell in charge of Bradford – where they went down, but we won't dwell on that point for too long thank you!

First game in charge. At home, the place where it all started for him. Against Middlesbrough, the team he used to manage........ oooh suit you sir! Did he want it sir, the three points sir......ooh

We journey to the ground with all the usual hyped up media attention. Paul Franks on WM is giving it big, Robson this and Robson that, and Tom Ross is giving it even bigger on 1152 going on about when he was here 20 years ago, but it shouldn't really take the teams attention away from trying to get a much needed three points from today's game. Recently this Boro side managed a comfortable win over Lazio so there should be no doubting that this is going to be a hard game with the likes of Viduka and Jimmy Floyd tearing the defence to pieces. However, with a new manager in place, the team will hopefully, have a more realistic view of the future of this season. Perhaps they will give their all for 90 minutes because over the last few games it seems like some of them are playing for their wages and not for the good of the club or the supporters. The amount of money some of these guys are on really does take the piss – and I'm not even going to start on about the top players' wages! (I've just read that John Terry has signed a new contract at Chelsea which puts his basic wage, yes just the weekly amount whether he plays or not, at 80 grand! That's only more than 4 times my annual income each and every week, and don't forget the extra add-ons, win bonus, endorsements etc etc..........) Sorry, I've finished now!

The game, well, what can I say? This must have been a brilliant first half "for the neutrals". End to end, chance after chance, we should have been given a penalty, and so should they really. Hasslebank hit the bar; Gera was on fire, shooting from all angles whenever he was within 20 yards of the Boro goal; and to quote mom's cousin Pete, "Contra has been a revelation up our end!" (He sits in the top corner of the East Stand, Brummy End – that's Pete who sits in the stand not Contra!)

After a series of attacks and some good football from the Albion, Downing broke down the left and after Hasslebank had wriggled past his marker he fired the ball across the goal. Unfortunately Darren Purse could only divert the ball past Hoult for a big fat O.G. – shit, it was all going so well! But credit to the Baggies, they kept their heads up and continued with the pressure on the Boro goal. Schwarzer had pulled off some fine saves before the opening goal and continued to do so, before another Albion attack shortly before half time saw Contra weave his way in from the right wing and put in a low cross for Earnshaw to slot home from close range – get in! Boing! Boing! Back flip, summersault, big cheesy grin, he's getting the hang of this at last! Now if it wasn't for half time, I think we might have gone on to get another, but when the teams started the second half it was as if the Albion players had left half their brains back in the dressing room! There was no pace like the first half, no aggression, no creativity, Boro didn't really raise their game –

they didn't need to – the Albion just didn't get going again!

Now I know that Robson had said earlier in the week that all the players would be starting with a clean slate and that if they showed willing in training, they would be in with a chance of a start, but where did Rob Hulse suddenly emerge from? I honestly can't remember the last game he played in, we probably lost, and I'm sure he didn't score! Nothing against you personally Rob, it's just that now we've got Earnshaw, Kanu, and the mighty Horse I wasn't expecting to see you on a Saturday afternoon team sheet in the Premiership. I suppose he must have been pretty good in training though, so we'll see! He was introduced with Horsefield with about 20 minutes to go and apart from one great chance where he just….. couldn't…. quite reach….the ball as Horsefield crossed from the right, he didn't do a lot to be honest!

Now you know when people say "Where were you when Kennedy was shot?" or when Princess Diana was in the car crash, well for the generation of 2004 that question will be slightly altered in years to come. I know it doesn't even remotely have the same meaning but the next few moments will haunt the Albion faithful for years and if we end up being relegated by just one point, well……. I don't even want to go down that road! "Where were you when Kanu missed from half a yard?" isn't exactly an international question but it really does have to be seen to be believed! I remember seeing Kanu playing for Arsenal on Match of the Day or the Premiership with Des or something, can't remember who it was against but it was the most outrageous piece of "skill" I've ever seen. I think it was Bergkamp who played a ball in for Kanu, from the edge of the box, for him to run onto. He ran past one defender, beat the next with a step over, and then beat the keeper with another step over, he got credited with the goal without actually touching the ball.

However, on this not-so memorable occasion, after some more good work by the new boy Contra, Horsefield played a perfectly weighted pass across the face of the Boro goal, everyone missed it and all that was left for Kanu to do, completely unmarked at the back post, was to side foot the ball into the back of the net……… not on this occasion! I'm sure he'll be asked for years to come how he did it and I'm sure he'll never really know, but somehow he managed to get the ball off the ground and up over the bar from only half a yard out. That's right, about a foot from the line he skied it over the bar – Savo style big time!

Fortunately, as Adrian Chiles is an Albion fan, we only had to watch it about three times on Match of the Day 2 and as Mr Skinner is an avid Boing Boinger, I don't think we'll see it on Fantasy Football too much if they do another series. I'm sure it will be on Soccer AM's Taxi slot for the rest of the season though!

Not an awful game by any means but there's not a lot you can say after seeing a miss like that.

I'd also like to add at this point, Mr Koumas didn't even make an appearance today! He came on as a sub in the last two games under Frank Burrows but with no real effect on the game. I'm not sure what's going on in his head but he had a bad run-in at the end of last season, didn't know if he was getting a new contract – which they gave him eventually, got a few unnecessary cards and missed the start of the season. But since he's had the chance to play he hasn't really grabbed the game by the scruff of the neck like he did 18 months ago or so! The last time he had a really good game was away at Forest last season where he absolutely terrorised them! Come on Jason! You know you are good enough – just show us – well show Mr Robson in training first.

Arsenal away

Arsenal away - you're having a laugh aye ya? The thought of this fixture just makes me smile to be honest. They have just finished a run of 49 games in the Premier without defeat. No, hang on a minute I just said 49 games - that's more than an entire season. Absolutely unbelievable. I don't particularly like Arsenal but the way they have been playing this season is close on perfection. Defensively sound, creativity in midfield and electric pace up front. The truth is, all ten outfield players are capable of scoring and beating a man, no joke and that makes them almost untouchable. Their performance away at Portsmouth in the FA Cup last year during their run was quite simply the most complete I have ever seen I think. They passed and moved at rocket pace, created chance after chance, showed exciting levels of skill and commitment and won 5-0. They received a standing ovation from the entire ground. Enough said. With all that in mind, plus our general play at the moment, I approached this game with a wink and a smile.

Gav stayed at H and Danny's so me and the Smiths headed for the

Library at 9am Saturday morning. We went through the England shambles in midweek on the way. The racism aside, I thought England were crap. It was the worst team performance I've seen from our national side in a decade (post Taylor). Rooney was berated for being petulant and disrespectful, he was hauled off before half time. He did behave like the kid he is and yes, he would have probably been sent off had it not been a friendly but I didn't agree with a nations outrage at his throwing away of the black armband in memory of Emlyn Hughes. Not for one minute did he mean any disrespect to Crazy Horse, he was wrapped up in a game of football and frustrated to the point of exploding at the pathetic service he was getting from midfield. There is no thought going through a player's mind as he is hauled off at the red mist point regarding an armband he is wearing. The public outrage should have been at the awful showing from the rest of the team who obviously wanted to be anywhere but in Spain. Friendlies get worse by the minute, players view top class Champions League games as more important, whether the old school like it or not. England caps are tossed out like pennies and we play too many meaningless matches for them to genuinely cause a tingle every time they pull on the 3 lions. Sad but true. The other worrying point to discuss from the night in Madrid was the racist abuse the Spaniards gave our Black players. The Big C received it in the 1970s but this was a different time, a different generation. I can genuinely say I haven't witnessed large-scale racist abuse on the terraces for years in this country. It was like going back in time. It raises an eyebrow when I hear it in the former Eastern Bloc, but lets face it, them lot are light years behind us in every aspect of modern life, but Spain? A liberal, Westernised democracy of today's EU - I was amazed. Their manager started it, however, with his comments about Henry and as the Spanish FA did precisely that - FA, the level of acceptance clearly rose. Fortunately, the world governing body FIFA was soon to step in and solve the situation. Or did dear old Sepp Blatter do what I knew he would - jack. I promise you now if this would have happened in England we would be playing behind closed doors for a year and we would have known about it an hour after the final whistle. My Dad always said to me that everyone hated us and we never get a fair deal. In this respect I know he is right.

We parked at Blackwater road and got the tube into Finsbury Park. The away guide said to head for a 50-50 fan mix pub called the Twelve

Pins (formerly the Finsbury Park Tavern). We hung around the station for a bit getting our bearings then Andy asked some bloke where the pub was. "Sorry mate, never heard of it". The boys crossed over then shouted back to me that they could see the pub just up the road. We got in and had a few beers watching the Man Utd game on one telly and the Norwegian version of the Auld Firm on another. After a bit I went to the bar and bumped into this bloke .. "Sorry mate" "no worries mate" - same bloke from the station who had never heard of the pub! Dickhead. We met Gav, Kate, H and Danny boy for a couple more beers then headed for the ground.

Walking down the street we saw the ground before us. No wonder they are moving to a new stadium - the turnstiles are literally in between the houses. The away end is like going up an entry in Ethel St Smethwick. I'm sure the occupiers of the flat above the entrance can see most of the game. The facilities at the Clock End for away fans are crap. How this passes safety regulations I'll never know - you could not move at half time beneath the stand. We found our seats towards the front left then it started to rain - nice. Another reason to move in my opinion. Why have grounds where you still have rows of seats where you can get wet? I heard someone call my name from the section on the side that they give you there and looked over. There was Shirl with his cheeky grin surveying the scene and his young lad in tow. He was banned for longer than a murder sentence the one year I played with him for The George but that's our Shirl. The game started and I looked at their team across the field. Campbell was missing but apart from that all the big boys were there. I don't mind admitting - I thought we were going to get tonked. First half was scrappy with no real threats from either side to my amazement. They had the ball for very long periods but it wasn't the walk over I feared. We played with Kanu (or Kan't do after last week) up front on his own with Earnshaw on the bench, this didn't exactly fill me with hope. When the half time whistle went and we were at 0 - 0 I was gobsmacked but part of me thought, no, fair play we deserved that.

It was brass monkeys I'm telling you so we tried to get a cup of tea at half time just to hold. The queues were ridiculous but after much pushing and shoving Paul managed to supply the hot drinks and cold dogs as they should be known down there. To the left of where we were sitting there was this corporate box of sorts right in the corner of the ground. All these suited gin and tonic tossers were taking the piss with their drinks and warmth and generally laughing at us, to which the Albion were not impressed. A small section surged towards the barrier and hurled abuse until the Police intervened. The game livened up on the hour when Pires, the French high board diving record holder attempted a curler into the top corner. Hoult had it all the way and managed to dive, half catch half parry the ball. It was up the other end so I couldn't be sure but replays showed the ball squirmed free as he landed and trickled into the net. I couldn't believe it. The funeral service hush of Highbury turned into a roar and the corporate box brigade laughed even louder. Well that's that I thought, might as well go home now.

The onslaught I feared failed to materialise and the Albion actually began to look almost the equal of our cosmopolitan hosts. I'm not saying we knocked it about like them or anything but it just seemed to me that Arsenal were either happy to stick with the one goal or we upped our tempo slightly. The rain continued as the night air bit my face - sorry I realise that last line was more suited to a Jack Higgins novel wasn't it? Basically it was bastard freezing, that's better. With about 15 minutes to go the ball looped up high towards the touchline, Greening gave chase to this seemingly impossible task. I watched as he brought it down over his shoulder into Ashley Cole's territory with sublime skill. He darted after it, whipped a wicked low cross under the challenge of Cole. I peered on my tiptoes into their box and watched Earnshaw move like a viper - bang, bottom corner - have that. We went barmy. The bloke in front of me grabbed me round the neck and jumped like a nutter, screaming down my ear. I freed myself to take my customary position in these situations and stood on my chair cupping the ears and generally giving it loads so the shiny shirt boys in the box could see. It makes me laugh to be fair. I watched this Albion fan surge forward then stand with his arms wide, nodding his head at this bloke in the box, blowing kisses and mouthing to meet outside. That split second of lunacy you feel when your team has scored - priceless and inexplicable to some but every footy fan knows what I'm on about. The last few minutes felt like a geological time period (that's a tremendous exaggeration) but then the man in black blew his whistle. The Baggies had drawn 1 - 1 at Arsenal. This was 15-1 in some bookies, the same odds of finding life on Mars I swear.

We crushed our way to the streets outside and skipped down the road. The Albion were so chuffed it was untrue, it's been a long time since I've heard us sing in the streets outside an away ground. "Can we play you every week?" and "Champions league - you're havin' laugh" made me smile. But one Arsenal fan with a large girth (fat git) wasn't too happy with our piss taking and started his own chant "Premier League - you're havin a laugh". 3 or 4 Albion fans then turned round and gave him loads back. This one bloke from Smethwick went "Oi, f**k off fatty" whilst another went up to him and gave him a playful slap round the face and poked his belly singing "f**k off fatty" whilst he danced on the spot. Sorry to say it but it was one of the funniest things I've every seen at a match. Seeing this Gooner spluttering "get off, get off" while another fully-grown bloke of about 40 poked him in the belly had me in stitches. We got back to the tube station after saying nevermind to Danny Boy and reached the car still laughing. What a day, what a result - is this the start of our season for real under the guidance of Captain Marvel? Man Utd at home next week - bring 'em on.

Man Utd home

Now let me think; what was it the bloke from T-Mobile said in the build up to this game? Oh yes, something like…

"Ladies and gentlemen, boys and girls, welcome to today's game. We are glad to be with you for today's game, which will see the official start of T-Mobile sponsorship of this club. Mr Woo is entertaining you again on the pitch with his ball juggling skills and he will return at half time. It is such a privilege to be sponsoring this club at this time with its new start under a new manager."

You see before kick-off there was Mr Woo doing his usual thing. (I wonder if Frank Skinner ever imagined seeing Mr Woo on the hallowed Hawthorns turf when he met him in South Korea?). Press-ups and sit ups while keeping the ball in the air, running with the ball on his forehead, all sorts of crazy stuff – why don't we sign him as a player not just a crazy mascot-sponsor type-thing? Anyway, while he was doing all that, there were T-Mobile people with jackets and posh uniforms and huge pink T-Mobile flags! Is this the final of the Superbowl or something? Far too over the top if you ask me! I wonder why they chose today to do it all official? Oh yeah that's right, new manager, new sponsors,......... and 50 million United fans watching around the world on MUTV!

The game kicks off eventually after all the razzmatazz has died down and as I expected, as soon as we make any slight contact with a United player, the ref blows for a free-kick. I wouldn't mind if there was a genuine foul or if the player was trying to con the referee, but no, nothing at all, just a case of getting on the right side of Mr Ferguson right from the start. There is a shout from further up the Smethwick "The Premier League......... Is f*****' bent! No let's not have that chant already; come on give it a few more minutes, it must have been the fourth minute before we heard it at Highbury!

Another typical start from the Albion. Very aggressive, not too much sign of respect for such a high profile team and end-to-end action, that's more like it! Unfortunately, Rooney is dragging Johnson all over the pitch, well Johnson is hanging onto Rooney's shirt more like; and Ruud, well, is just being Ruud in and around the box. Standing off side for free kicks and corners and confusing the hell out of the Albion defenders, and then to top it all off Giggs tearing strips off Scimeca every time he gets down the wing. On the other hand, Contra is again playing very well attacking Heinze at every opportunity, and Moore and Purse seem relatively strong at the back.

Sorry, famous last words and all that! Within the space of about 10 minutes towards the end of the first half, Contra has to go off and then so too does Big Dave a few minutes later. Not sure exactly why either have been subbed, but it must be due to injury – they were easily the two better Albion players in the first half hour. Tommy "With his leadership in the Premiership" Gaardshoe slots into the defence and Robinson makes an appearance pushing Clement back into midfield. Sakiri had started today's game instead of Kanu, partly perhaps, due to his good performance at Arsenal and possibly because Kanu might have picked up a winter back injury, which will put him on the sidelines till, ooh, March at least! No only joking Nwankwo, not sure of the change to be honest! Sakiri's doing all right again though!

In the second half there was another major combination. United stepped up a gear, mainly down the left where Heinze was now more free to roam with the departure of Contra; and the Baggies really didn't seem to turn up for the last 45. This soon led to more and more pressure from United and the inevitable finally happened ten minutes after the restart. Heinze to Giggs, Giggs to Scholes. I wonder what happens next? You guessed it; Scholes strikes from just inside the area, one nil – so obvious really! Fifteen minutes later another needless free-kick given away on the edge of the box. Giggs crosses, Heinze out-jumps Sakiri (which wasn't hard, come on Artim!) and Ruud-boy heads the ball across the line for the visitor's second goal. Come on Albion, at least make them work hard for the victory. Horsefield came on for Sakiri half way through the second half but unfortunately the damage had already been done. Even though there were some flashes of excitement for the home crowd, United really started to turn the screw. With Keane and Scholes really grabbing the game by the scruff of the neck, Rio Ferdinand must have felt like he could have stayed in the dressing room for the second half! I'm not saying we did nothing second half, but I'm sure a United back three could have easily dealt with the minor threats at goal. A short spell of 18-yard pinball between Giggs and Wes Brown, a clearance by Robinson and then back in by Rooney, enabled Scholes to bundle the ball home from a few yards out. I think that's well and truly game over now then! I think that makes us bottom. Oh well, we can only get better from now on then??!!

Portsmouth away

Now I apologise again for getting on my high horse after the Crystal Palace game and ranting and raving about the state of Selhurst Park, but can I now vent all my anger and frustration from almost one of the worst ends to a football match I have ever seen. Well, no actually. The more I think about it, I would still have written most of the following comments but if the ending of the game had been different I wouldn't have to write this through gritted teeth!

In true Selhurst-style, where shall I start, I honestly don't know. The journey was ok actually, Kate's car working like a dream down the M5, A34 and M27. The pub wasn't bad either, walking distance from the ground – which always helps – and Sky Sports! After a couple of beers and Chelsea v Newcastle on TV, we stroll to the ground to be confronted by the towering floodlights of Fratton Park. It's my first visit to

Pompey's ground; please note the word ground and not stadium, definitely not stadium! We pass several burger vans which don't get much better as we near the ground – I'll wait until inside – and I'll use that term loosely too! To get to the away section we pass behind some houses along a wide alleyway with graffiti and corrugated iron either side of us, where are we Beirut?

All I can say is, at least it's not raining today? Why, I hear you ask? The away end of this dump is uncovered! (Sorry Ken Sandel if you're reading this but I've got to get this off my chest – and you probably haven't been in the away end!)

OK, now then, if you can just picture this in your mind, I can't be bothered to draw a little diagram; two turnstiles then an exit gate; then two more turnstiles; the food counter and then the gents and the ladies toilets. Yep, you got it, all in a line!

Now that bit where I said "I'll wait till I get inside", the only bit actually inside, or undercover is when you're actually in the toilets, which are right next to, as in not even six foot away from, the food counter. Which itself is about as big as a McDonald's drive through, and I'm only talking about the hatch where you order your food! Food, well, I had some dodgy grey looking burger which didn't have much consistency as I was eating it so, I'm not sure how my bowels will cope – apologies if you're about to eat!

Now to top all of this off, you've got people coming in through the turnstiles wanting a piss or wanting some food and not knowing a) which queue is for what, b) where they are, c) how this can pass for a Premier League ground or d) more importantly, if we are going to get wet today, let alone take home three points?

Aaaahh! That's better, now I can sit down in our almost front row seats – trying not to scrape my shins on the back of the seat in front or knee someone in the back when we start to attack - and try to enjoy the game. Row 4 to be exact and I was smack bang in the middle of the goal. Great view of the back of Houlty for most of the half.

The whole game was really a comedy of errors for the next Nick Hancock's Footy Gaffs Collection. First of all Pompey concede an own goal after about ten minutes, as a stray boot rifles the ball into the back of the net from an Albion cross. Then Darren Purse decides he can try the same, if not better, by crashing the ball the wrong side of the post, leaving Russell Hoult with no chance. But Albion did deserve to go in at half time in front and with only seconds remaining in the first half, the Portsmouth keeper decides to come charging out of his goal towards his left hand corner flag. Between him and his defender, they fail to clear the ball and Greening is able to cross the ball for Earnie to slot home from a yard. Boing Boing! Have that!

Second half we actually did something that we haven't done now for a few weeks, which is start playing again! Against Chelsea, United and Middlesborough especially, we just haven't looked like we were playing second half. No shape or creativity or aggression or anything, but today we kept things simple and straight forward without really going to get the third goal which would have killed the game off – perhaps we should have done! All afternoon the Portsmouth faithful had been crying out for free kicks for this, that and the other whenever there was the slightest chance of a foul. Well on this occasion five minutes before the first victory under Bryan Robson, the ref gave in to the home crowd pressure and awarded Pompey a free kick. Ok, no prob, Big Dave and Pursey you know what to do, just head it......... too late, that De Zeeuw has almost a free header to steer the ball into the back of the net! Come on lads, never mind still a point to play for, or just go down there and sneak another goal. Perhaps not, Earnie's not on the pitch anymore – Robbo's having a look at Mr Hulse!! Bryan you can have a look at him in the club shop, there's bound to be a picture of him somewhere in there! He just isn't good enough at this level on the pitch – sorry, enough is enough!

Two minutes to go, a point each then, fair enough! Oi, Clem, put your arm down and get on with...... I don't believe it! Lua Lua has just got their third! Don't stare at the linesman, just concentrate on staying with the player you're supposed to be marking, you idiot! No points now! Time to go – sick and tired of watching shit like this! It's sooooo frustrating! I don't think a player should get paid when things like this happen! 2-1 up with five to go – shocking! Now you understand why I said I'd be writing this through gritted teeth!

Two years ago there were some similarities between the first weekend in December 2003 and this one in 2005. Yes, I know the Albion were in the relegation zone and we were playing away (Spurs then) but do you remember what happened on the "other" day of that weekend? It was the never-to-be-forgotten, mammoth excursion on behalf of

Langford's Tours. Yes we went on another Beer Trip to sunny France. With shopping lists in hand, ferry tickets at the ready and a fart machine which needed batteries, we set off for Dover; this time we remembered the passports before we departed and had another enjoyable but not quite as tiring journey across the Channel. Perhaps not another two years before we go again, eh?

Charlton home

Still reeling from the last five minutes of the Pompey game I looked at this fixture and thought surely we can get something here. Charlton Athletic - you are joking right? I mean just saying the name makes you laugh. I suppose other fans round the country say the same about the Albion but Charlton? Please! Their manager is worth his weight in gold. Look at the facts, their support is reasonable at home but even that is boosted by 4000 away fans and 5 London derbies so gate receipts can't be a major factor in their finances. What I'm saying is Curbishley has spent very little but Charlton are seen as an established Premiership side. They have no real stars to talk about but season after season produce enough results to keep them comfortably in the division. A miracle to me I must say. I say without question also that the Albion are a bigger club than Charlton. My problem, however, is convincing others and I'm beginning to see their point. How much longer can we harp on about trophies won in yester year, crowds we have, potential this potential that. Truth is we no longer have the right to say we're bigger than Charlton just as Burnley can no longer hold a torch to Blackburn. It's today that counts and today we are bottom of the league in a worse position than two years ago when it was all a big adventure.

We headed for the George at half twelve and popped in the bookies just before hand to study the footy odds. Said hello to Bano who loves his horses then chose two from each section. I soon realised that this weekend for the fixed odds was dire. London derby, Merseyside derby, Birmingham derby, East Midlands derby, Lancashire derby and so on. In short, the odds were shite and I found out later that trying to pick results was a waste of time. We had a couple in the George with a turkey and stuffing bap (you know) then Vince drove me and Tez to the ground. You know when you could cry with the pain of wanting a jimmy? I got out the car and wrote my name up the wall in seconds. I didn't really but remember that at school? When I heard the team I thought a ghost from the past had took charge for the day. Our right back come midfielder Scimica was playing centre half whilst Gaardsoe, a centre half warmed his backside on the bench. Nice touch. Charlton FC brought their typical away following – 200, which is pathetic and annoys me to the point of exploding. They took 2000 to the closest derby of the season at Palace last week. We took nearly 4000 two weeks earlier – say no more. The crowd was announced as usual and them two bob fans from Greenwich actually had the nerve to go Ooohh to take the piss. Let me just set the record straight here, the reason we didn't sell out is the same reason you see a boat load of blue seats behind the goal on MOTD – we allocated big club Charlton the best part of 3000 seats and they could only sell ten rows, end of story.

The first half was dreadful. The second half was worse. I'm struggling to remember if we kicked towards the Smethwick End first or second. Anyway it docsn't matter because it was the worst Albion performance I've seen in a good while. Matt Holland scored the only goal of the game for them on the half hour I think after Johnson failed to connect with his clearance – there's a shock, he didn't NEARLY do something did he? Jesus this is ridiculous. The boos rung out at half time and the natives were more than just bloody restless I'm telling you. But for a brave second half display at the Library and a ten minute spell at Portsmouth the Albion have been awful. Not bad, awful. We have ten points. We had more than this last time but hadn't spent 10million quid. The second half dragged and dragged and the faithful began to lose their faith. In fact towards the end it got moody in the Smethwick as some blokes vented their anger vocally towards players and Robbo himself whilst a few "die-hards" (idiots who can't have anything said against the Albion, however constructive it may be) visibly and orally disagreed. "F*ck off you w" "come on then you twat come down here and say it" etc. etc. and so it went on. The stewards moved in after a while and actually formed a human barrier at the end to avoid confrontation. It was that bad. Fans fighting amongst themselves. Awful I know but it means so much. You want your team to perform so badly it hurts and when they look like a Sunday team, well the frustration boils over. The final whistle went and the boos echoed around the half-empty ground. The atmosphere was terrible and I felt a real turn in attitude amongst the fans. Something told me this was gonna be one long season ahead but poor old Robson seems incapable of changing our fortune. I want him to succeed so badly just like most Blue Noses must have done with TF. He and the Big C were my heroes as a boy so to see him fail now at "home" is not nice. Blues away next week - can hardly wait!

Listening to Talk Sport in the week I heard Karen Brady going on about the plans for a new super stadium in Brum. I'm sure I heard her use the figure 60 000 for the capacity, she then went on to use words like corporate entertainment, state of the art facilities, national and international functions, casinos, leisure complex, etc. etc. Not once did she mention Birmingham City FC. Made me realise a few things - football is certainly not what it used to be, the Blues are run by business people (soft porn and now gambling business people), their aspirations are on a different planet to our own and more importantly Brady hasn't got a clue who BCFC really are. Oh well, if it comes off they'll have a lovely half-full stadium to play in once a fortnight.

Blues away

Now I don't know if you knew this but with the proceeds of the last book I bought a Vespa PX 125 - you know. It is simply beautiful, my pride and joy. I always wanted one as a boy but could never afford one to be honest with college etc. so I thought no, I'm doing it. I love being on it and have a permanent rye smile when I'm speeding along because I know, well I like to think so anyway, that lads over about 25yrs and girls actually too, look and think "yeah man, that's the ultimate cool". Open faced helmet, green Parker, etc. you can shove these pathetic Suzuki scooters the Kevs taz about on, this is the real deal - retro cream and brown too. Anyway, enough salivating over my Vespa, the reason I'm saying all this is because me and Gav had the idea of going to an away match on it together and this was it.

Alot of planning went into this journey I can tell you. Gav was meeting me at Tez's garage at 10.15am (early morning kick off) and Smithy at 10.30. I was to put the cover in Smithy's car and we would sort of follow each other down Hagley Road to our parking spot. We would put our helmets in his car and put the cover over the bike (it has WBA on the front!) then head for the ground. The planning paid off as it worked a treat. Going down Hagley Road (not a minor road son to be fair) Saturday morning before Christmas on my Vespa with Gav on the back was such a laugh. The looks we were getting made me smile. I like to think it was because we looked so cool although I'm not too sure. We went round 5-ways island which is our Arc De Triumph island in Brum with our eyes shut going Aaaahhh all the way round. A coach then decided to pull out on us and I thought I would never stop so gave him loads of abuse to which he politely replied ... "F**k off". I pulled up by the Mosque in the wrong lane after coming out of the underpass tunnel next to a pick up with 2 Blue Noses in. The window came down, "Alright lads, going to the match ... "yeah" .... "Get in there, good luck, you're gonna need it, ha ha ha, etc." I thought yeah shut up mate and let me pull in front of you - which I did. We then stopped in traffic at the big island on an incline and as I pulled away Gav's weight went back and we wheelied (if that is a word) up the road like Evil Knievel. We parked up and covered the bike, leaving our helmets with Smithy (no jokes please). I was relieved to be honest but we had a proper laugh.

Thinking about it that was the highlight of the day and where the laughter ended. We went in the ground and queued for the 3 days to get a beer. I spoke to "access all areas" Malc and assured him they had nothing to fear from the Albion. 2 minutes in and we gave away a blatant pen but Riley waved play on thank God. 2 minutes later and he evened things up with the home crowd by pointing to the spot after Purse wrestled with Morrison and he fell to the floor. Everybody's favourite Robbie Savage stepped up and placed it in the bottom corner. 4 minutes gone and we are one down already. At this point I just want to discuss our team with you. Robson started with centre half Gaardsoe in midfield again and utility man Scimeca, centre half. Haas came in from nowhere at right back and Kan't du was on his own up front. Cunningham and Upson must have thought it was a charity match such was the threat we posed. We did actually create an opening pretty soon after they had scored when Gera hit the bar, but that was about it to be honest. Morrison made it 2 then Heskey 3 and we hadn't played half an hour. Paul turned to us and said he was off. He disappeared and like a scene from a daft comedy film, returned 5 mins later hunched over with his hands in his pockets ... "Got no bus fare". Here was a bloke who had to watch his team because he didn't have the means to get home without his bro - we did manage to raise a smile over that. The Blues had stopped piss taking and the atmosphere seemed to turn to pity rather than anything else. How low can you get? Pity from the Blues.

The second half was no better even though Robson brought Earnshaw on (our top scorer) and actually played with 2 up front - too late mate. Horsfield, the ex-Blue Nose was left on the bench for a game that was perfect for him and Robson simply lent against the dugout, motionless and seemingly resigned to our fate. The Albion fans must have had enough by this stage as pockets of them began to sing things like "Lets pretend we've scored a goal" and "Premier League, we're havin' a laugh". Now let's get one thing straight right now. I would not have sung that if you begged me. We were playing Birmingham City for God's sake not Man Utd. I wasn't havin a laugh I was livid. My team were being pissed on by the Blues, they were laughing at us and some idiots in the Albion section thought it was okay to enjoy themselves. Are you totally mad? I seriously couldn't endure much more and was looking for the way out. Then something occurred which kind of catapulted me to the exit amongst hundreds of others. Robson brought Ronnie Wallwork on. I'm not too sure I need to say anything else to be honest but non-Albion fans may be reading this too so let me explain. Wallwork does 100m in the time it takes Pluto to orbit the sun, okay slight exaggeration as it's not 248 years but you get the message. Secondly, he hasn't been anywhere near the first team for about 2 years and finally his performance away at Wimbledon (MK) a couple of seasons ago was the worst by a midfield player since Geoff Thomas tried that lob playing for England. He replaced Haas which was cheered by the fans and then when his name was read out they jeered just as loud - it was that kind of day. I headed for the exit in disgust and bewilderment, shaking my head. We will end up with fewer points than 2 years ago, having spent millions and less than the Dingles last year, who were ridiculed from the first whistle. The fans chanted for the Horse, asked Robson what the hell he was doing and even lorded Megson.

My Vespa was still intact even if my pride was not. We shot back home through the streets of Brum still managing a smile. I loved Robbo as a player for his complete commitment to the cause but I'm scared he will be remembered as a failure and hounded out of the club where he first made a name for himself, such is football.

Liverpool home

Today for me started as it probably did for most people around this time of year, nursing an enlarged stomach and a sore head from the previous day's experiences. Either too much to drink, or too much sitting watching TV, or too much noise from new toys and family gatherings; and to top it all off, too much food! Even though you're not in the slightest bit hungry, and you've eaten enough to feed a small family in Mozambique for a week, you stand there, leaning against the wall, pint in one hand, talking to a family member you haven't seen or spoke to since last Christmas. Meanwhile, your other hand is, without any thought process whatsoever, moving from the bowl of nuts to your mouth several times a minute. When the nuts have finished you simply start on the next bowl..... Pringles!

In the olden days of the 40's and 50's, the games played over the Christmas period were always the games involving local teams, the derby games of the season. This is a great idea if you ask me, all the local rivals would be able to play each other in the build up to the new year and then on New Years Eve, we could beat the crap out of those whose team had just beaten us, instead of fighting with – or trying to throw punches in the general direction of – the bloke who you think has been trying to chat up your bird all night and you've got the wrong end of the stick because you're a bit drunk! A more logical reason for a brawl if still a stupid one!

Onto a more entertaining thought, its Liverpool today and I'm sure you don't need reminding what happened last time they visited the Hawthorns! Well there's no Owen this time so hopefully the score might stay respectable – but then again they have got Garcia, Alonzo, Baros with a back up artillery of Gerrard and Riise's missile collection! Oh well!

Bottom at Christmas, has, in every Premiership season so far, meant down at the end of the season. Now if I'd had got a tenner for every time I'd heard or read this phrase in the last two weeks, I think I could have helped the Albion find the right man in the forthcoming "January transfer window", who would not only keep us up, but would push us into the European places! Well he might have come from Europe, but I would have been comfortably well off over Christmas, I can tell you. Apparently, his royal highness, the Lord Chancellor of all things defensive, Scottish and Scouse has announced to the nation that "he vowed never to write anyone off, but I'm writing West Brom off." Cheers Captain Scarlet, but I'll wait till it's a bit more mathematical thanks (or when we don't buy anyone in January like last time)!

Albion started well and after seeing a few of Gerrard's long range efforts go over the bar it was Horse's chance to attack the visitor's box after a poor clearance. Unfortunately Hyypia produced the tackle of the match (with only ten minutes or so gone) to deny a shooting chance from inside the area, never mind Geoff, you didn't do anything wrong really, keep your head up! Then Gaardsoe evened things up with a great tackle on Baros at the other end. Gerrard then took centre stage again to supply the on-rushing Riise with an inch perfect pass to open the scoring. That didn't stop us from continuing to try to play creative attacking football – why is it, we always play better football against the better sides and then when the likes of Grimsby (ooh just the mention of that place sends a shiver down my spine) and Rotherham are in town we play absolutely shite – with Koumas and Contra both creating chances for Earnshaw. The problem is with Liverpool and most other top sides, however many chances you create yourself and don't put in the back of the net, they will always look like adding to their tally when they've got Pingy-pongy-wots-his-name running around up front not giving our boys a second on the ball. To make matters worse, from what should have been an Albion free-kick shortly before half time, Liverpool break, win a corner and Contra decides he'll go in goal for a few seconds instead of letting Hoult collect a relatively easy catch at the far post. No hesitation from our beloved Mr Styles and Contra is yet another player to be sent off for the Albion this season! Just what we need when we're already chasing the game!

Second half went, again, from bad to worse but remarkably ended on a strange note! Liverpool unfortunately managed to find the back of the net on four more occasions which after the other day at Blues is going to make the goals against column look like a cricket score. Ping-pong scored and so did Gerrard but his tame, but curling free-kick should easily have been stopped by either the wall or Houlty himself, and after Riise claimed his second of the game, Benitez decided enough was enough and brought on Luis Garcia, you guessed it – he got number 5! Now for this strange note; for the last five or ten minutes of the game, large sections of the Brummie and Smethwick Ends were chanting the players names and singing Albion songs as if we were the team winning, not the team on the end of another Liverpool humiliation! I know it sounds silly but I can see why – in a way. Last time round when Liverpool were cruising, it was as if the players had given up, Gerrard was playing like he couldn't be arsed and it wasn't even halftime! On this occasion, yes they were losing, but they still looked like they wanted to win the ball and do something attacking with it, when they had the chance. However, I couldn't really bring myself to join in with the singing or applauding them off at the final whistle. We lost 4-0 last week and now 5 so can't really see the point of applauding anyone! Hulse came on for Earnshaw for the second or third time since Robson took over – it's surprising what a new manager sees in some "out of date" players isn't it!

I don't think Mr Hansen will change his opinion after watching that game!

Man City away

After some careful negotiations with Mrs Langford (that's Fay not Janet), plenty of chocolates and flowers, and whispering sweet nothings in her ear, Stef has managed to obtain the newer of the two Clios associated with Elm Croft. More realistically, Fay was probably still getting some serious kip when it was time for Langford's Taxi Services to pick up the faithful few - that's me and the twins (that's Andy & Paul, not Clive & Jon)! After negotiating the traffic on the M6 north we reached the inner sanctums of Manchester and the "delightful" area of Mossside.

As we approach the ultra new, ultra modern City of Manchester Olympic Stadium – to give it its full title – we notice another site for our more cultural readers. To the untrained eye, this piece of modern art is simply a metal palm tree that has been stuck in the ground on the piss and left to go rusty! To the trained eye, it may still look like that but it is actually there to represent something! "B of the Bang" is there to symbolise the moment when a sprinter starts their race according to Linford Christie, something to do with leaving the blocks as soon as you hear the gun firing and not after it has fired!! Anyway, back to the football. After attempting to park in the away car park and then Stef remembering about when Malc had parked there for the Blues and couldn't get out till after the coaches had gone, we decided a side road would be better if we had to leave early! Ah, secure parking on a school playground for £4, that will do nicely! Remember what I said about the area earlier? Well say no more! As we leave the parking area, the car park attendant calls to us,

"…There's an Asda over the lights if you fancy some food or need some money lads…."

"Cheers mate, wot about pubs? Where's the best place for a drink?"

"You wanna go in The Crossroads or Mary Ds but don't go in the Queen Vic.

They'll f***** shoot ya!"

"Ok cheers mate!"

Something tells me we won't be going in the Queen Vic for a pre match drink!

We took up our positions in Mary Ds which, considering the time was about half one, was fairly quiet for a pre-match drink. Ah, I know why! No sky sports on big screens, always a crowd puller! We settled at the one end of the covered pool table, considered about asking for the cues for a game and then considered the possible repercussions – think we'll leave the pool today! After a few beers we head for the stadium. They don't use the usual paper tickets now at Man City, oh no not in the Olympic Stadium. But they haven't quite gone the whole hog of Style cards like the Baggies. You get these shiny cinema style stub ticket things that you show to a bar code reader which lets you into the ground. Paul questions the steward on the entrance,

"Can we get out early if we have to mate?"

"Yes mate but no re-entry"

Look mate I don't think you quite get what we're on about and if you hadn't noticed we're not astronauts! I don't want to come back and get my coat out of the car if I'm cold, we really mean if we're 3 down at half time is it time to "do one"? The way we're playing, we could be 3 down in ten minutes but that's the Albion for you at the moment.

Inside the ground it is exactly what it is, if you get what I mean, it is an Olympic Stadium (Commonwealth really). Olympic standard catering; Yes there's the usual burgers and beer if you want it but there's also salads and pasties and baguettes and all sorts of bollocks, ready for any Tom, Dick or Harry who walks through the doors – turnstiles – for an international event. Olympic standard toilets; not quite Olympic sized but plenty of room for waiting your turn. No reason to use the sink, disgusting, like I've seen at some places! Olympic standard space in general. Plenty of room to wait around, with fifteen minutes to go before kick off it felt like it was about half one because there was so much room. The only thing it did let itself down on was the Ladbrokes stand. Man City must have been hosting Bolton on their last home game because the information about the match odds was still up on the walls. Considering we were in there from just after two o'clock, the woman didn't come to the stand and change the betting sheets till about ten to three, we all knew what we wanted to bet on so there was going to be a big rush during the next few minutes. Ever the optimist, I went for something like Gera first goal, Albion 3-1 or something ridiculous. We hadn't scored three goals in a game all season and Man City didn't exactly let in goals for fun these days, but you never know!

As the game got going and took its shape, City were obviously the more creative team and Robson had set his stall out with a bank of 4 defenders and 5 across the midfield. At least we would try to prevent the opposition from scoring a bit more than games of late. As Fowler broke through the ranks and headed towards goal Gaardsoe gave us an idea of why he didn't play more rugby. It was a poor rugby tackle and a very poor football tackle to say the least; more of a half hearted grab and tug challenge! Fowler goes to ground on the edge of the box and out pops the red card from the referee's pocket. No complaints – stupid Gaardsoe! In the last game Contra was sent straight off for a silly handball and now another needless red. The free kick was wasted and Albion reshuffled their pack with Clem dropping back into defence. We held our own for the remainder of the half, not really creating much but not letting City have too many chances either. Just before half time the ref awards them a dubious free kick on the edge of the box and Anelka curls one into the top corner leaving Hoult no chance of stopping it. Half time, one down and down to ten men. Just keep going lads, it could be worse!

Second half is of more concern than the first. Hoult is playing a blinder and stopping everything they shoot at him, but we're not really creating anything for Horse up front. He's giving his all tracking back when needed but then we hump a long ball up to him where he's either never going to reach it or he can't hold it up long enough for the midfielders to join the attack. Frustrating but not much you can do when you're a man down. Some sections of the supporters are getting on Robson's back chanting for Earnie and trying to get Robson to make a change. We don't look like scoring and this is frustrating the fans more and more as the game goes on. With fifteen minutes left on the clock, we decide that as it's cold and wet and it looks like we've lost this game we'll depart early. We'll go on the second goal, or if Hulse comes on I say sarcastically – as if Hulse will come on before Earnshaw! Robson does finally make a change with about ten minutes to go. Guess what? We're out of here. Hulse is getting stripped off. As he makes his way to the touchline, we depart from the ground just managing to see Gera coming off in his place. What's all that about, eh? Surely if you're bringing Hulse on you're trying to get a goal, Yeah, so why take off Gera, surely Wallwork should have come off, he looks knackered anyway! Then as we get across the main road we hear a cheer, which must be the second for City, but it's not as loud as a 40,000 strong cheer would be. We reach the car to find out that Earnshaw has come on for the Horse. Our attentions are now drawn to the radio for the remainder of the game. Shortly after coming on, Earnie has caused enough worry in the City defence that Richard Dunne and David James have a right mix up in the City area. A long ball is punted up field and usually Fatty Dunne (as I like to call him after his shit performance at the Hawthorns when we beat them 4-0) would touch it back to James or leave it for him or even control it himself and start a new attack. Not on this occasion and believe me it has to be seen to be believed! I only wish I could have seen this from inside the ground because it would have been right in front of us. He tries to control the ball while facing his own goal. You can already imagine what's going to happen, can't you? Somehow he gets it all wrong and manages to control the ball as it bounces up and hits his shin pad. The ball bounces off and completely wrong foots James who is left stranded towards the edge of his area. An own goal it is despite "Fresh legs" Earnie's chase behind Dunne towards goal in an attempt to get the last touch.

I suppose in the end we'll definitely take a point to help our lost cause, as some Scottish/Scouse pundits have written us off already. Well we were the bottom club at Christmas and no Premier team has survived if they were bottom at Christmas! We'll see then shall we! There's a challenge if ever I heard one – what do you think Robbo?

Bolton away

New Year's day - oh what joy. I once said this was the worst day of the year and to be honest, I haven't really changed my mind. The day after the night before and all that. I must at this point refer to the festivities last night. We all went down the Wernley for the lovely disco and had a laugh but I must discuss a meeting I had with the one and only Simon Rees. I hadn't seen him for about 5 years to be honest, he had moved to Burton with his girl so our paths didn't cross. Previous to that he was part of Brandhall Rovers FC so I had known him years. Si is a legend. He has various nicknames - Fat bloke, Pieman, and BS, all very complimentary aren't they? He is an artist by trade but has spent most of the last 10 years in construction, prior to that he found it difficult to follow the right career as the demand for his art work was slow coming and well, to be honest reading the paper all day seemed far less effort. His stories are legendary like his £900 pearl necklace and the building of the Wesleyan in town, so seeing him again after all this time made me smile. Apparently he didn't have a ticket but when he pointed out to the doorman that he had drank enough beers in this place to by his house cash, he was soon aloud in - know what I mean? Say what you like about Si his heart is in the right place - after all, he did save Sanita's life when he was a lifeguard.

Smithy picked me up at 9.30am and we went for Gav. The M6 was clear and we headed for the NW in quick time. After breakfast at Knutsford we made our way round the various Manchester motorways and were at the Reebok for 12pm. We parked up and headed for the pub. Now the Reebok is new and really that's the kindest way I can describe it. I've been here quite a few times but it never actually impresses me and I really mean that. From the outside it looks plastic and unfamiliar. The floodlights do it no favours at all and inside it doesn't get much better. The seats are arranged in a semi-circular fashion but this leaves lots of useless space but that's just my opinion, I dare say the Bolton fans love it. We reached the bowling alley pub we frequented two years ago but the barman told us away fans were not allowed in - nice. We went to the next pub to be told the same by the huge doorman - if only Fat bloke was with us I thought. We eventually found the Beehive ten mins from the ground and had a couple in there. It was some kind of kids pub with no TV for the Liverpool Chelsea match so the lads were not particularly impressed. As we left the pub it started to hammer down. I was the only one who didn't leave his coat in the car so smiled like a Cheshire Cat as everyone else got drowned. We queued for the "food" for 15minutes to be told there were no pies left but for cheese and onion and beer was not to be sold - best wishes BWFC and all the best for the New Year.

After about 10minutes it rained so much Forrest Gump would have been impressed. I'm not joking it rained boy and made me think of the recent tsunami tragedy in SE Asia. I suppose events like that put it all into perspective to be honest. Here I am all distressed and annoyed because the Albion haven't played well and then I go home and hear that another child has become orphaned or a single family member of 12 is the only survivor - I ask you?

We started quite well in awful conditions and put Bolton under threat straight away. They have been going through a real bad patch to be honest and have fallen like a stone after the heady heights of 4th place and talk of Europe. Europe? Bolton? I hear Majorca is nice for an end of season Beano. After about 15mins the ball broke to Gera with his back to goal 25 yards out. He spun instinctively and ran with the ball across the edge of the box, hitting a low curling shot that skidded into the corner of the net passed the outstretched arm of Youth Team keeper Kevin Poole. Okay you spotted it, he is about 50 years old. 1 - 0 to the boys - we boinged in the wind and rain like it was a Mediterranean beach. Ten minutes later Horsfield was clean through but he screwed his effort into the side netting when 2 - 0 would have probably sealed it the way they had been performing of late. Somehow I just knew that miss would come back to haunt us. The rest of the game was poor but Bolton controlled much of it and things looked ominous. 15 mins left and Robbo pulled off another of his inspirational substitutions. Albrechson replaced the lively Greening who was out on the left wing with plenty

This isn't mine... it's for Paul

Didn't have this problem on the Vespa

I honestly thought this was a prison

10ᵗʰ April 2005 93mins 38secs

One minute you're up...

...next minute...

Is it Brighton away today?

I told you it would rain!

Hat-trick hero

Has anyone seen where coach 4782576 is?

There's only one...

Feed the Horse and he __will__ score!

The Three Amigos

I love it when a plan comes together

left in his tank. Now the Dane is a centre-half / full back at best so to play him wide left made me frown somewhat to say the least. The obvious switch was Koumas for Wallwork considering Ronnie had touched the ball about ten times all game, okay he never gave it away but he was blowing out of his arse after an hour. 3 minutes from our first win under Robson and away from home that barbarian Campo played the ball inside the poorly positioned Albrechson (shock Robson) and the ball was squared for of all people Diouf to hammer into the roof of the net. 1 - 1 and I went back to Horsfield's miss in my mind but found no comfort at all to know I was proved right. The Senegalese striker went barmy and made it quite clear to the Albion he had scored - we had been booing him and giving him abuse for his spitting incident a few weeks ago. Now don't believe me if you want but I tell you now, I'd rather a bloke punch me than spit in my face like he did against Portsmouth the other week. The thought of that makes me sick, dirty bastard. It's okay for onlookers to make comment but I promise you if he had been smacked in the jaw by De Zeeuw of Pompey for doing that he would have deserved every thing he got.

Anyway, we held on in the last few minutes for a change and took a point from the Trotters - what the hell is that all about Del Boy? We got back to the car and only waited a few minutes before we were off the carpark and away. I say that because before the game when we returned to our car for the coats the money grabbing swines had packed all the cars in they could so an early escape was way out the question as we were blocked in by about 5 cars. Luckily for us we were by the exit off the carpark because I heard afterwards a bloke had been on there for over 45minutes waiting to go - I'm sorry Bolton Wanderers but that is a disgrace.

Newcastle home

It was bloody freezing. We kicked off at 8pm for Sky TV reasons, which I wasn't too impressed with considering our record live to the nation. Newcastle were without Shearer, Kluivert, Bellamy and Malcolm MacDonald so we had a chance some thought. Tez had Fay's ticket and we all met in the Wernley before hand for a couple of beers. We got in the ground in plenty of time for a bet, Vince had Newcastle to

.

win 4 - 2, which I thought was nice. The team was announced and I had to get confirmation from the lads that I had heard right. Wallwork still the general in the middle, Kantdo, Earnshaw and Horsfield all up front and no Koumas. The midfield had no creativity in it at all and the front 3 didn't have a clue who was doing what or why for that matter. As Vince always says... Robson doesn't do himself any favours does he? Where he got that formation from only he knows and the Lord himself.

Not surprisingly we seemed clueless going forward because Horsfield drifted out left and Earnshaw right naturally - neither of which are wide players and it showed embarrassingly for Earnie in particular. Horsfield did, however, wriggle free from Bramble (who doesn't?) half way through the first half but the keeper saved - again, that was our chance! It was more hustle and bustle than the beautiful game but at least I felt interested and not cringing or having to listen to in-house arguments for a change. Newcastle didn't fill their allocation surprisingly but when I thought about the weather, the distance, the time of kick-off and the fact that it was on TV I couldn't argue with some empty seats to be fair. I purposely watched Earnshaw in the second half and ended up shaking my head so many times it was untrue. He is a 6-yard player, a box man, one touch finisher and nothing else I'm telling you. Gary Lineker once said he had good movement, now I don't know whether he had seen him in Brannigans up Broad St dancing to YMCA or something but from what I saw second half his movement was crap. He called for the ball with his arm aloft with 2 defenders around him and the ball player 40 yards away. He then proceeded to jog with the 2 defenders while our bloke ran down the line looking for a cross. No near post run, fake, dummy back post, double back whatever you want to call it. Then when he did get the ball out wide or on the edge of the box he ran with it head down, into players or had a wild shot, which threatened the scoreboard. Play him up front and tell him to hit the box running for God's sake!

The game wore on without any real incident but it still held my belief and interest far more than in recent weeks. I genuinely thought we could get something from it, even a win. Newcastle out passed and manoeuvred us in midfield with the impressive Jenas and determined Bowyer making them tick. Ameobi was their sole front man but he still caused us problems with his movement and strength. As the game headed for the final stages I just couldn't see either side scoring but never admitted it aloud as you know the Albion will let you down when you least want them to. The game passed with little more incident and did finally end up goaless to my relief and surprise. We were now unbeaten in 2!! We are on a roll, a run if you like - okay stop laughing.

I got back home and watched some episodes of The Office. I don't know whether you have seen any but it makes me roar. The one when Brent's branch has been taken over by the swarve bloke from Swindon - Neil who takes exception to some comments Brent said to him in front of the rest of the workers. They go in the office and Neil gives Brent a rollicking to which he says very little and they shake on it. He comes out afterwards and tells the others…..

Brent: "did you hear any of that in there?"
Others: "no"
Brent: "phew, I tell you not nice man"
Others: "why, what did he say?"
Brent: "slagging you all off man"
Others: "no, really?"
Brent: "You should have seen me I told him straight"
Others: "Did it get nasty?"
Brent: "he would have come through that wall if it did"
Tim: " I dunno, Neil seems pretty trim to me"
Brent: "against karate?"
Gareth: "do you need any help if it happens again?"
Brent: "Na man, this is big boy shit"

I was laughing for ages. Then there's the one on staff training day when Brent plays his guitar…. "Free love on the freelove highway.." with Gareth closing his eyes and harmonising while the guest speaker sits and stares in amazement. Then Gareth asks Brent if he is going to release his song …. "Well it was recorded ages ago man, if I released it now I'd have to slap on some drum and base shit with it".

My sister sent me a text the other day, her son Max said to her, "Mom why do people laugh when I say West Brom?" She replied "because they don't score many goals", he said "I could help them" - he is 4 years old and has the rest of his life to look forward to following the Albion, poor kid.

Fulham away

First of all, I would like to say that before kick off at today's game, I genuinely thought the Albion were playing away in Europe somewhere! I know the fixture was against Fulham but I can honestly say that I have never seen so many foreign people at a football match in all my life! I'll try to explain my point.

Due to today's game being the third match out of the last five of Albion's games to appear on Sky (and Man City next week is on Sky as well), the Smith's decided that based on the last few performances and a 4.05pm kick off on a Sunday afternoon, The George would be a better place to watch the game rather than on the banks of the River Thames! So it was left for me and Stef to venture forth to the Capital of England and mingle with the foreigners. Don't think that you are overwhelmed by Cockneys in London! No, no, no! All bloody foreigners. Illegal and legal immigrants, Black, White, Asian, plenty of Oriental folk – I think they're the leftovers from the Inamoto fan club. He's actually an Albion player now you know, but unfortunately he hasn't started a game for the first team since signing – with a broken leg – back in the summer. Now for the real twist in the tail, he's gone to Cardiff on loan for the rest of the season! How does that work then?? Sorry off on a bit of a tangent then. We follow the signs for White City off the A40 and then head towards Putney Bridge. With the ground set amongst the houses to our right, we now had the impossible task of finding a place to park! Streets of house everywhere, which these days mean streets of Residents Only parking spaces. By shear coincidence more than anything really, we decided to try a turning on our right. Fantastic no Resident la-di-da and we squeeze the car between a Vespa and a mini – rapid! After a short walk between the houses (bit like Coronation Street) we approach the ground. Oldy-worldy cottage in the one corner, hence the name of the ground, which they have kept even though they have modernised it in recent years.

Anyway, yeah all sorts of colours and creeds! I definitely heard a few German voices and French and Spanish! But what was confusing us most of all was the fact that some of the supporters had Fulham scarves and jackets. Were we in the right place? We looked around to double check for any signs. We saw a sign that confused us even more! Away fans to the left – ok so we're in the right end; Neutral fans to the right –

what the f***! Neutral fans! What club in their right mind have neutral fans? Well obviously Fulham! Now I know people down in this area of the world tend to be a little better off than most but how does that work? Neutral fans? I really am struggling to get my head round this one! Does a Chelsea fan wake up on a cold January morning and think to himself: "hmmm, after that convincing victory yesterday by my beloved Blues, I think I'll go and watch Fulham today"? And even if he does, why does there have to be a section for Neutral fans? Surely they could just pay for a home ticket and sit with the rest of the supporters?

On a more geographical note, I think this ground is actually closer to a river than Shrewsbury's ground so as Stef quite rightly pointed out before kick off, as this ground never gets flooded, it shows what a good job the Thames Barrier does – I just thought I'd throw that one in for discussion! And just to make matters even more confusing – the home fans, who sit towards the away end in the stand which backs onto the Thames (are you following this?) have to walk under the away end to get to their stand! So as well as the "neutral" Fulham fans, there are also "home" Fulham fans mingling with the away fans – I wonder if they'd allow this for an Albion - Wolves match?

As well as the usual procedure for pre-match entertainment, we have tried to make the game more enjoyable if not entertaining by having a flutter or two on the first goal scorer and result of the game. Not as easy as you may think, I can tell you! Kate keeps telling me to just give the money to her and I'll definitely win in the end – Yeah but it's not the same is it and Nan would have let us and we all know how she used to like having a go on the machines! On this occasion, a notice on the back wall caught our eye as we lined up to place our bets: Campbell to score 1st goal, WBA to win 2-0 100-1 £10 bet gives £1010 return. Our eyes must have lit up like Christmas trees! Fiver each and no more bets thank you! We venture to our seats and admire the few hundred neutral idiots who probably don't even know what country they are in let alone which ground! I'm sure I just heard one of them say, "where is West Brom any-way??" Tossers! Before kick off I rang my mate Neil to see if he had got to the ground ok. He'd made a slight misjudgement and come down the M1 instead of the M40. The traffic for our short journey after the motorway seemed excessive for a Sunday evening so I don't think he's going to make the kick off as he's still in north London! A few minutes later I get a text from him: Not goin 2 game now. In pub in N London called The Albion. Loads in here. Even got Baggie Boys and Baggie Girls on bog doors! At least he'll see the kick off now.

The game itself was one of the strangest I had seen for a long, long time. After Earnshaw could have had a hat trick in the opening ten minutes and somehow failed to make any of the chances count, Campbell was put through one on one. We both jumped off our seats wishing the ball would hit the back of the net – it didn't! Edwin van der bloody Saar managed to get a hand to it as he shot towards goal and then moments later managed to smother Campbell's second attempt at goal. This is much more like it Albion – just stick it in the net will you. Campbell ideally but anyone will do. We can definitely win this game; I don't think Hoult even touched the ball in the first half hour! The second half was the same as the first really, better if anything! It's definitely starting to click with Robson at the helm but I just hope it's not all too late in the day (well season!). Campbell seems to have fitted in to his new challenge, linking up well with Earnshaw and the midfielders. With most of the Baggies attacking players having shots during the course of the second half, Van der Saar was again the busier of the two keepers, it must have been a good game – even AJ's shots were on target! Van der Saar was finally beaten by a Wallwork shot which deflected off Campbell's heel. Again we leapt to our feet willing the ball into the back of the net. Unfortunately for the Albion and our bank accounts the ball beat the upright too. Are we ever going to score today? During today's game we went down the usual list of away day songs - My garden shed; Shit ground, No fans; You're only here cuz it's Albion; We all follow the Albion, to name a few. Today, however, we heard a new one for the first time. Mr Ronnie Wallwork has been honoured with the latest addition to the Baggies song sheet! To the usual tune…

"There's only one Ronnie Wallwork,
One Ronnie Wallwork,
He used to be shite, but now he's all right,
Walking in a Wallwork wonderland!"

Unfortunately, AJ was taken off after an hour, injured rather than subbed! A rash challenge by Boa Morte left him in agony on the turf and he was eventually stretchered off! He has played very well lately, forming a commanding partnership with the Mighty Wallwork! Campbell was "nudged" on the edge of the area shortly before the end of the game but to be perfectly honest there wasn't much in it – the papers and reports and even Robson were saying we should have been given a penalty – he should be stronger than that really in my (and Stef's) opinion! Now for the Hollywood style twist and for those with a weak bladder – what, no sorry! Those with a weak heart; don't watch any re-runs or highlights of this game. In fact if you're not feeling up to it, just go straight to the next game, no seriously………..

As the seconds ticked by and the fourth official held up the board to display how many more agonising minutes we had to endure this dom-ination without a goal, a rare Fulham attack gave the home team an even rarer corner. No prob – let's just clear our lines and head home with a point, it's not what we deserve or are duly entitled to (three points for an impressive display if you ask me) but it will do. Ball comes over; heads go up, all except for Mr Clement who has done admirably at the heart of the defence for the past few weeks. Unfortunately, this leaves a free header for Mr Papa Bouba Diop – yes that is his real name! He times his run to perfection and plants an unstoppable header past Hoult – I can't believe it! Stef can't believe it, I'm sure Clement can't believe it, and I know Robson can't believe it either! Let's just say that a few choice words were vented from the mouths of probably 99.9% of the Albion fans at the game and probably from a higher percentage watching the game on Sky.

We drove most of the way home in silence, speechless, in a mild state of shock really!

Man City home

Out of my brain on the 5.15. No not the train to Brighton but the Albion's bizarre kick off time on Saturday night. After last weeks torture at the hands of all things foreign down by the Thames, this was a game we had to win if we had any glimmer of hope. Last weekend saw a change in the wind, in the wind that blows through the ranks of Albion die-hards. Robson is now beginning to gain respect. When I think back to that day at St Andrews and the stick he had to endure I never thought I would see it but I have. His name was sung at Fulham for the first time since his first game in charge - clear indication of happy times. You know what? I was so chuffed because as I have said before, I want Capt. Marvel to succeed so much for everything he means to WBAFC. He is even sticking to a formation and regular players! One thing I can't quite truly believe yet, however, is the re-emergence of Ronnie Wallwork as a footballer. More of that later.

I had a beer in the George before the game and me, Gav, Vince and Fay headed for the match. Man City filled their allocation, which they always do to be fair and the atmosphere was building. I backed the Albion to win 2 - 1 with Earnshaw 1st goal at 50-1. We started really well with Campbell winning most things in the air against fatty Dunne and £5m Distin (that has to be joke, right?). £40m rated Shaun Wright Phillips, who is tipped, incidentally to push Beckham out of the England team was strangely quiet. We broke down the left after about ten minutes of snow and wind through Greening who whipped it across to Campbell who hit it first time - bang 1 - 0 Albion. We went barmy. City had been piss taking about relegation but had gone well quiet now. The ground boinged and the Lord is My Shepherd rang around the stands. We continued to press and looked really comfortable against a City side who were without Mr Loyalty himself, Anelka but still boasted Fowler, Wright-Phillips, James and McManaman, etc. Everytime Wallwork did something I shouted Ronnie - playing like a young Beckenbaur in his prime. The fun was beginning to creep back into home games!

The second half was pretty similar but I just knew we needed a second goal to see off any threat from City. They really are the strangest of teams Man City. They are the only team to have beaten Chelsea this season yet here we are running them ragged and making them look ordinary. Supporting the Albion is bad enough but following Man City must be a bloody nightmare. Each time Dunne had the ball the cries of shoot went up - just after Christmas we went up there and were battered for 90mins only for Dunne to score a howler of an own goal late on to give us a point. Kevin Keegan and Man City are a match made in heaven or hell depending on your point of view. They are perfect for each other - one minute you're up beating Chelsea, the next minute you scoring OGs for bottom of the table West Brom. One minute you're European footballer of the year, the next you're seen in Spain with a big beard - you see where I'm coming from? There is no in between with either of them it seems.

Midway through the second half Horsfield replaced Earnshaw, he was not too hp to come off I tell you but he had little argument. His first touch was dreadful, his runs lacked any intelligence and he gave the ball away and shot wildly. Robson said afterwards that Earnshaw needed to work on his all round game outside of the box - understatement of the year! At one point he had a chance to out run Distin after a City corner - he got to the ball first but his first touch went ten yards straight out of play into the Halfords lane at about 100mph. It was simply incredible. With about ten to go we passed and moved sweetly down the left for Greening again to centre, the ball was headed back to the diving Wallwork, yes I did say that, to nod home past England's number 4 to make it 2 - 0. We jumped around like nutters - I got on my chair and sang at the City lads who were now left in total depression. Surely the game was won now. The Albion sang Wallwork's name but probably not as you would expect. We heard it at Fulham last week but the majority of Smethwick Enders hadn't - "There's only one Ronnie Wallwork, one Ronnie Wallwork, we thought he was shite but now he's alright, walking in a Wallwork wonderland". Believe me that is complimentary I swear. With a few minutes to go City had a free kick on the edge of our box, the wall lined up, Poll backed off, then Dunne ran up and smashed it into the roof of the net. They went mad but probably madder when they saw Poll holding his whistle in the air and motioning to take it again - he hadn't blown his whistle!! I just laughed to be honest, this really was our day. The final whistle sounded and the Baggies had won - you beauty. I was so chuffed.

You know when things happen that make you stop and think it doesn't really matter? Well, my mate Vince has got to go to his Mom's funeral on Monday after she passed away last week. She had been really ill for years to be honest but it still doesn't alter the fact that she has gone. He is just a regular lad who lives a regular life just like you and me but facing this would test the best. He knows I'm really skint at the moment so on the quiet without anybody knowing he handed me a bunch of notes before the game - that's the type of friend Vince is. He is the best and I will be there on Monday for him.

Crystal Palace home

Well folks this really could be it! We have to win this game, no, I'll re phrase that; we need to win this game, no better than that, we must win this game! Palace are starting to put a bit of daylight between themselves and the relegation zone and even though it is only a couple of points, tonight is an ideal time to not only collect some much needed points, but to claw them back towards safety. After the narrow defeat at Fulham and then heroics against Man City, we should be able to brush aside this one-man band outfit of a team! On Mego's fateful trip to south London, Andrew Johnson destroyed our afternoon without having to try too hard, so surely with a bit more fight at the back and the new found confidence in the players we should be well up for tonight's game! There is a slight change to the formation tonight and Robson has decided to change the front two as well! For tonight's game, me and Kate have been moved to wide right; no we haven't signed a contract, we've just swapped seats with mom's cousin Pete Webb and his daughter Dana who have season tickets in the East Stand. It's a cracking view from almost the back row (and we're right on the edge of the 18yard box), not sure if Kate's ears will hurt on the way back down though – bit of an altitude problem you see (she needs to pay a visit to St James' Park!).

If you thought the Fulham game was a little tense, well please keep your arms and legs in the vehicle at all times and remain seated until the pilot has switched off the seat belt signs – you're in for another bumpy ride! This is the Albion after all and to polish things off we've got the ever-popular Mr Dermott Gallagher in charge! We start off brightly, as usual, with a few shots from Gera and big Geoff, Gera's effort going inches over the bar. Shortly after this chance, Horsefield was put through and as the Palace defender challenged him on the edge of the box, he inevitably brought the Albion striker crashing to the ground. Now I've seen worse challenges go un-noticed, but on this occasion Mr Gallagher used the "ridiculous" letter of the law and showed him a nice shiny red card, which glistened in the evening rain and was a delightful sight for the blue and white faithful. Right lets get a hold of this game! Ian Dowie reshuffled his pack and set his stall out again leaving Johnson on his own up front. Apart from a shot from Campbell, we didn't really create many chances over the next ten or fifteen minutes. This was partly due to the fact that when Albion are playing against ten men, they just can't seem to break them down, and what wasn't helping was that every decision or foul seemed to be going in Palace's favour - I think the ref may have regretted sending the player off!

As the half time whistle approached, the Baggies started to create more chances; Purse headed wide and after Gera had shot just wide of the target, it was Campbell who should have scored with a free header from a Purse cross. On the stroke of half time, Greening thought he should have had at least a free kick on the edge of the box when Powell pulled him back as he was in full flow. I know you're not going to send another bloke off ref but surely a yellow card? Ref? Hello? That foul... just then... On Greening... the one where he had his shirt pulled back as he was running into the box.... I know you were giving them loads of decisions in the first half but come on ref that was a blatant foul! As you can probably guess, we didn't even get a free kick and as the players leave the field for half time several of them are questioning the ref on some of his decisions (nicely put or what?).

Not sure what Captain Marvel must have said at half time but we started the second half with our brains in the changing rooms I think! Hoult, Purse and Clem all at sixes and sevens as a ball is punted up field from the Palace keeper. As the ball is coming down to earth, Purse and Clem don't seem to know who is going to header the ball and who is picking up Johnson. Two seconds of confusion later and the ball is in the back of the net! Hoult had come off his line and instead of heading the ball away, Purse ducks underneath it presumably because he heard a call from Hoult – or maybe Johnson shouted something the little you-know-what! Anyway, as I said Johnson nips in between and nods the ball over the advancing Hoult. One nil down, this wasn't supposed to happen! It took us what seemed like forever to get back into the game and Campbell thought he had scored after the Palace keeper failed to hold onto his effort on goal. The ball rolled along the front of the goal and onto the far post. Unfortunately no Albion players could react quickly enough and the keeper smothered the ball at the second attempt.

The game was looking lost and the gap above us to safety was looking bigger and bigger. Robson decided to throw on Earnie and Kieran Richardson to try and liven up our possession. Then with probably ten minutes left on the clock, Gera sent over a cross and after confusion in the Palace defence the ball looped up over the keeper and Campbell was on hand to scramble the ball over the line at the back post. Get in there! Emotions were expressed but not with the same enthusiasm as the usual Smethwick End way – I'm in the East Stand remember and more importantly I've got a 70plus year old bloke next to me! If I start jumping around and hugging him he'll probably have a HA! Hold on a minute, he's probably been watching the Albion since before I was born so if he was ever going to have a HA it would have probably been around.... Oooh.... Let's say around the 90s during that brutal Buckley/Smith era!

Campbell lead the troops back to the centre circle urging them on to go for the winner. Palace couldn't complain really they had done nothing all game and had only really scored because of a defensive mix up. As the minutes ticked by and the fourth official showed us how many more agonising minutes we would have to endure, Campbell slotted a ball through to Earnie who managed to chip it over the keeper and into the roof of the net – let's just say I forgot about who I was, where I was, and who was next to me for the next few seconds! At last a victory in the dying seconds and not a defeat! I think Earnie was still celebrating as they kicked off, but as they hoofed a free kick towards our area, some of the other players must have still been celebrating too! A back post header which wasn't cleared by a Baggie boot was directed into the top corner by an outstretched Palace leg – oh dear is the polite way of saying what 90 per cent of the crowd must have been thinking and as we kicked off the ref blew his whistle for full time. I know they say you're at your most vulnerable when you've just scored but come on lads, we scored in about the 92nd minute, just concentrate – please?

So with everything all square, there isn't any change in the table – we're still bottom but hopefully we can do better at Norwich on Saturday because if we don't then, without sounding like a complete defeatist, I think we're down!

Norwich City away

Now I don't know whether you know this but Norwich is bloody miles away, basically you head east in a straight line and just keep going till you come to it. The A14 is a main road obviously but when I tell you it has nearly 40 junctions you get the picture. Norwich are just above us in the table and like us, tipped for an automatic return to Div 1. They are hard working with little creativity and don't score many goals - exactly the same as Palace and us I suppose. This was a vital game to be fair for both teams as Palace had lost in the morning kick off so a win would put you right in touch with the last Holy Grail safe place.

The girls had gone away for the weekend so the boys were free baby. I went out Friday for a drink then Vince and Gav picked me up and we stayed at Gav's. We went to bed about 2am, hammered. Vince slept on Kate's side (don't tell her) and I was in a bag on the soft floor - softer than Gav's bed anyway! I woke in the morning to find no Vince in bed - when I checked down stairs there he was under my coat in a ball - "you bastards were snoring like a pair of walruses". We shot up the Albion to get tickets for Spurs away in the Cup next weekend then picked the Smiths up. Before we left for the Albion Gav farted in his kitchen and I have never heard anything like it in all my life. I genuinely thought a dog had barked it was so loud and was fully expecting his stomach to be sucked into his ribs so much air came out of his ass - dirty get, I was drinking a cup of tea too!

We headed east as I have said already and just kept going. Breakfast at McDonalds was a good call for a change but added to the Chinese we ate last night and the thought of the food yet to come it wasn't the best in hindsight. We eventually got to Norwich for midday and headed for the ground. We parked on a multi-story and walked out into a kind of Brindley Place setting - bars and restaurants by the river, pedestrianised and quite up market. Nothing like the ropy dives we have been to so we were well impressed. We had a few in Wetherspoons then Old Orleans before heading off to the ground. Smithy had 2 burgers outside the away end so was called a fat bastard much to the amusement of David Bentley who was also in the queue getting his hot dog (hope Arsene doesn't know). We got in the ground and the other Smith had 2 pies, fair play Delia, he said they were well nice but having an exclusive Shiraz on the beer menu was a little over the top love. Norwich have a nice stadium to be honest, not too dissimilar to our own. We were on the side and quite high up but it was a good view. That was until these couple of kids came and stood in front of us all pissed up and wanting to fight the home fans from their seats and singing every Albion song going. He looked at me and I said sit down son, a bit like Clint Eastwood all moody and controlled - he sat down, don't mess with me!!

We were playing really well again, like we were leading upto the Palace shambles. Knocking it about nicely and looking quite threatening. The ball broke down our left and Earnshaw was onto it like a flash. He out-sprinted the yellow defence and toe ended under Green to make it 1 - 0 Albion after about 15mins. We went barmy. I had 1 - 0 Albion Earnshaw first goal so was looking at a few quid at this stage. We continued to pass it and move with Greening looking lively and their defence all over the place. Then on the stroke of half time they won a corner. It swung over and the heads went up, it was half cleared to the edge of the box (surprise that) and knocked back in. No worries though, keepers ball all the way. Hoult came out to punch but didn't get off the ground. He was out jumped by their player. Hoult is 6ft 3in and was stretching his arms in the air too - I don't need to say anymore do I? The ball was flicked back into our net to make it 1 -1 with virtually the last touch of the half. Norwich hadn't been anywhere near the pace of it and yet were out of jail because we couldn't defend once again. I was angry to say the least.

Second half saw us take the game to them once more. I was well shocked to see us come out playing good football after conceding a sloppy goal right on half time. The impressive Richardson, on loan from Man U was dominating in the centre of the park and making us tick. Earnshaw picked up the ball in front of us and went past the full back. He whipped in a low cross and Richardson hit it home after a rebound off the bar, 2 - 1 Albion and time to go wild again. Me and Vince hugged and fell about the isle like nutters, giving the home fans behind the goal as much abuse as could be mustered. Don't ask me why and looking back makes me cringe but in that moment of uncontrollable joy that follows a goal I behave like a lunatic for want of a better word. We were in the driving seat again and they still looked easy picking at the back with little threat up front. Ten minutes later they get a free kick wide left. The ball was whipped in with pace and curl and as soon as it entered the box I knew it was gonna cause mayhem. It was one of those crosses where the keeper doesn't know whether to come or not and the defenders are equally unsure (Man U v Chelsea Carling Cup Semi at Old Trafford the other week?). Anyway, Doherty jumped for it and got the merest of touches leaving Hoult stranded. The ball went straight into the bottom corner 2 - 2. I just couldn't believe it. Our defending at set pieces is shit.

Plain and simple. Somehow I just couldn't see us going ahead for the 3rd time in a game we should have won comfortably. As time went by our chance of taking the vital 3 points seemed to disappear in front of my eyes. Then with about 5 minutes to go they won a corner - surely not I thought. It was swung over and once again only half cleared to the edge of the box (will we ever learn?), waiting there unmarked was their centre midfielder who smashed a volley past Hoult into the back of out net. The ground erupted as they knew they had got out of jail and won a game they were never in. Tears and outbursts of abuse that stemmed from shear frustration were the only things to break the silence in the Albion section. One bloke seemed intent on smashing the chair in front of him to pieces with his boot, perhaps the sight of the girl cowering into her dad's arms on the seat next to the one he was booting put him off. Then there was the irate bloke who said every swear word you could ever imagine, spitting each one towards the pitch, out of control, lost it. Others were slumped in their seats, heads in hand, shaking in a pitiful state, in shock, like a crash scene. I stood there with a mixture of rage and sorrow bubbling inside. Albion are the best and worst girlfriend you could possibly ever want all in one, the most addictive drug you could ever take - seriously you are as high as a kite one minute and as depressed as you could ever be the next. The final whistle went and I simply shook my head and turned to the lads - come on, let's piss off home.

We got back from the east so late it was untrue. Me, Gav and Vince stayed at mine so we drank to forget, till we couldn't see eachother anymore and then went to bed.

Southampton home

It's official in my opinion - we are doomed. We should have played this game last Saturday but we had an FA Cup replay away at Spurs to deal with then so this game was re-arranged for tonight. Snow had fallen all day so it was bloody freezing again come kick-off. By the way the FA cup game in case you were wondering - we lost 3-1 after being 1-0 up for the entire first half and playing Spurs off the park only to concede a dodgy penalty in first half injury time. Sound familiar? Albion playing well, not taking chances then defensive errors gifting the game to the opposition - about the size of it lately! All the lads went down to London on the Saturday afternoon for the 5.30pm kick-off. We were staying at Luton airport after the game and flying out to Amsterdam on the Sunday for Gav's Stag. Me, Gav, Vince, the Smiths, Scouse and Carl all had tickets for the Spurs games and were paying the Dutch capital a visit the day after, we met Danny Boy at the ground - Arsenal fan so wanted Albion to win more than me I think! Albion did our heads in once again but we soon forgot about that once we hit the hotel bar that night.

We got to the airport in plenty of time for the 1pm flight. Then Gav said it's not on the screen son so I checked the paper work again. We arrived in Amsterdam at 1pm, our flight was 11am. I couldn't believe it. My heart sank as I approached the Easyjet desk - "sorry too late for that flight, I'll check for the next one". We were in the airport 20mins before the plane took off but they wouldn't even try to get us on. Luckily, the woman said the next flight was not full so we could get on that, it went at 3pm so not too bad I suppose. We arrived in Amsterdam early evening and after messing about with trains and trams etc. we found the Hostel Annemarie in the dark. The bloke on the desk was stereotypical beyond belief ... "Hey maan, hows youse doin? Just sign this maan, hey that's cool maan, if you wanna little smoke just open the patio maan, it's cool". Our room sent me straight back to school and BB cottage weekends - big room, ten bunks, one toilet and shower, orange light, etc. basically Fay would have burst into tears once she had opened the door. We loved it. We spent the best part of 3 days and 2 nights playing darts, pool and cards, drinking laughing, flying and eating very healthily. This one bar was so seedy, if that's the right way of spelling the word it was untrue. We paid to get in then walked up the stairs into this dark room with a red glow. There was a long bar type feature in front of us and a cushioned-like area behind that. 4 ropy looking women paraded the cushioned area wearing nothing but a false smile each. Blokes took it in turns to massage the girls and watch them perform private sessions. I saw a banana at one point then it disappeared completely - fair play I thought, she does magic too. A few things I will remember about Amsterdam... Never agree to a full English breakfast from a Hungarian bloke who likes Marlboro, don't expect to feel normal after you have been in a coffee shop, animals should be kept in Dudley Zoo, don't share a toilet with 8 blokes, Carl doesn't drink, I have no idea where any museum or art gallery is and never eat a second hand banana.

Southampton predictably hit the ball long to the hideously named Crouch who invariably flicked it on for the speedy ex-Dingle Camara. By the way it made me laugh last year the way the Wolves tried everything possible to keep hold of him - they even rigged their player of the year award so he won it in an attempt to keep him at the club. He went to Celtic as soon as the last balloon of the end of season party had popped. The first half was poor but again we had our chances to go in front but didn't take them. Campbell was non-existent but now has the bloody armband so will never be dropped! The second half was no better but it still frustrated me to think here was a game with 3 vital points up for grabs at home against a poor Saints side and the Albion played so poorly it was untrue. We were missing the drive and energy of recent games and made very little in the way of chances. Camara continued to scare us with pace but his final touch in front of goal let him down thank God. Southampton were well supported to be fair for a night game midweek and sang "Harry and Jim ..Red and White, Harry and Jim ..Red and White" to which the Albion responded "Rosie and Jim .. Bag of shite, Rosie and Jim .. Bag of shite" - I smiled at that to be fair. The game ended goaless and I walked off shaking my head. I know every fan in the land says if only this and if only that but seriously we have thrown away so many points it's beyond belief. Pompey away - 2-1 up with 10mins to go, we lost 3-2. Norwich away 2-1 up with 15 mins to go, we lost 3-2. Palace at home 2-1 up in injury time, we draw 2-2. Bolton away 1-0 up with 5mins to go, draw 1-1. Southampton away 2-1 up 3mins to go, draw 2-2. Notice how the majority of these sides are in the same fight as us and yet here we are gifting points to them like we're some kind of charity. By the way that's 12 points in those games - we'd be in the top half!! I know what you're saying, it counts for nothing now but it does do your head in all the same.

Blues home

Sunday kick off at noon to avoid trouble - yeah right. Although our second city neighbours are going through a bad patch to hear them talk, they still beat Liverpool a fortnight ago and should still have enough to brush us aside I thought. Now the Baggies had just come back from a trip to Florida to improve moral - team bonding. The next time I have a shit lesson I'm gonna ask Keith the same question! I texted Malc before the game suggesting he went up the avenue behind the Smethwick as I was certain the Albion would close the gates before kick off that separated the away fans from us. We walked up to the ground to find the gates wide open - oh well. Outside on the corner were loads of lads just hanging about - I knew they were Blues a mile off. Caps, checked scarves, mobiles and smart gear - you know the score. The ground was pretty full before kick off but little atmosphere was being created. There just seemed to be an air of inevitability amongst the fans - we're down, Blues will probably win and are mid table and that is that really. They were thinking about the Villa next week and we were, well just there I suppose. Gav was on his honeymoon - bad planning that son so Carl (no beer thanks) had his ticket.

We started like a greyhound to my astonishment and soon had Blues on the back foot. Earnshaw was on the bench as Robbo had gone for the Horse against his old club - clever I felt for a change. He pulled the hapless Cunningham all over the place for 90 mins. Kieran Richardson, our on loan teenager from Man Utd ran the middle of the park again making the ineffective Diao look so poor it was embarrassing. The Albion asked all the questions and had at least 3 good chances to go in at half time 1 up. Blues were so poor I just could not see them being that bad again second half so willed the Albion to score while playing so well. Their full back, Tebilly I think it is, was woeful and I mean that. The thing I remember most about him was once in the first half he got the ball in his own half and under no pressure at all, moved forward and simply blasted it as hard as he could - it flew over everybody and went straight out of play for a goal kick. I actually laughed out loud. I promise you now, if I had done that on a Sunday morning I would have got a right rollicking. As much as we pressed we couldn't find the break through so went in at half time 0-0. I texted Malc saying I fully expected them to come out a different team second half and win 1-0 as we had now missed our chance again. He agreed.

Second half started and once again we went straight on the offensive. I couldn't believe what I was watching. Okay, Blues were poor but we must take credit for that too. We chased every ball and moved it quickly - they never settled once and created very little indeed. 10 minutes in Gera did superb to keep the ball in play and won a corner. The ball was swung over and an unmarked Clement rose to head down into the net - 1-0 and we went barmy. For the first time in a very long time we actually got something we deserved. Blues nearly equalised with their only real attack soon after as Heskey, (get up) headed against the upright. Not long after and Greening crossed for Campbell to volley home number 2. It was beautiful. I still expected them to come onto us and show that never say die spirit that has served the Blues well in Derby games anyway, but it never came. They booed them off at half time and trudged for the exits early. Malc said he had no complaints - the best team won on the day. I was just peeved we hadn't gone on to hammer them 4 and gain some pride back for that Christmas humiliation, but you can't have it all. The Blues sang "We'll meet again" as a reference to our relegation so we reminded them of their trophy cabinet, that still remains empty of anything but dust for over 100 years. The sun shone and we skipped down Halfords Lane. People were still talking of survival but for me that went at Norwich some weeks ago now. I might have listened had the Blues put up a show against Palace last week but they didn't, so catching them now is unrealistic if not impossible. Nice touch of the Blues to give Horsfield a standing ovation I felt at the end. They were angry to a point but this was a nothing match to them really. Their next home game in a fortnight is far more important than an inconvenience against us Yam Yams - Aston Villa. I know who I'll be supporting that day. On that note I was chuffed we won for a few reasons, one of which is I am pretty certain now that Villa can't send us down on the 10th April because if they could have, I wouldn't have gone as that would stay with me for life.

Chelsea away

Nice game in hand this one I thought - Chelsea away. I mean they're only romping the league above Arsenal and Man Utd, have already won the League Cup and just brushed Barcelona aside in the Champions League. It couldn't get any easier could it? All the talk at the moment is of their Portuguese manager - Jose Mourinho. He has breezed into the English game with an arrogance and style that has followed him ever since the first whistle. He gained immortality last season by leading the much unfancied Porto to Champions League success - a feat to be fair that you have to admire. History will not say, however, that they should have gone out to Man Utd after Paul Scholes had a goal disallowed when it was quite clearly well on side but such is football - they never looked back from that moment. I kind of dislike Chelsea because of their hideous spending power to be honest, but successive managers have spent a king's ransom on the Kings Road but have achieved very little for it in real terms. Jose is different. His eye for the right type of player to win the Premiership must be admired. He took over Chelsea when they rightly had the tag of big time Charlies - players on huge contracts who were not exactly up for the fight midweek in December away at a freezing Bolton for example. When the sun shone at the Bridge and all was well they came out to play and whipped most in front of them but when it mattered most, they hid and so Chelsea were left trophy-less come May. Jose sent Crespo and compatriot, Veron to Italy, Jimmy Floyd went to Teeside (similar destinations) and others followed out of the door as he obviously weeded out those he felt unable to fight for the cause. This you have to admire. He introduced a work ethic that perhaps had been missing from successive Chelsea teams and instilled a never say die attitude that Fergie would have been proud of. The result? Chelsea lead the title race by a mile and have their fingers in a European pie after already landing a domestic one. They play with flair on both flanks - Duff and Robben terrorise like Giggs and Kanchelskis once did, they are organised by a leader in Terry and an engine in Lampard that could rival Hansen and McMahon, Drogba has the brawn of Mark Hughes whilst Gudjohnson has the poise and craft of Bergkamp, their keeper, Cech, has a presence similar to a young Schimichael and their full backs go forward whenever they can - in short they have champions in each position.

I admire Jose for what he has done to Chelsea but still think he has a lot to learn. His reaction to defeat in the Nou Camp was churlish to say the least. His behaviour after Gerrard had scored an own-goal was simply out of order, say what you like about Sir Alex and dear Arsene but they would never run the touch line gesturing to the opposite fans to shut up. Jose is a good manager but he must learn how to lose with dignity before he is considered great - sorry, that's after a bag full of titles and cups too! Losing with dignity - not sure it will start here however, with the visit of my beloved Baggies.

Chelsea dominated the game from the off to be honest and had their French forward, Drogba been on form in front of goal we may well have been on the end of a good hiding. He did manage to convert a centre from the marauding Duff after half an hour to put them 1 - 0 up, however and although they didn't add to their tally it was a bit of a one goal drubbing if you know what I mean. We huffed and puffed as ever and played reasonably well. Robbo even went with 3 up front!! None of this lone striker business away from home for us but we still didn't look like penetrating their defence to be honest, although we did have 2 disallowed for offside (miles off but I still gave the lineo stick). We gained credit and respectability at the final whistle and Jose showed us his winning respect as I like to call it - I wonder if he would have embraced Robbo and spoke about us so kindly had we had knicked a point? Oh well no points from this one but didn't expect any either. Is it right to think that or should you be more positive? Dunno really, just seems funny to lose only 1 - 0 to Chelsea and listen to plaudits about heart and commitment, problem is the table hasn't got that in brackets after our points total. Time is running out, I still feel it's too late for survival, put it this way, if we stay up it will be the story of the century but I just can't see it. Oh well, Charlton away next week - how the hell are they in touching distance of Europe, and don't say the Channel Tunnel.

Charlton away

So this is the official start of the "Great Escape" is it?? Free travel on 40-odd coaches paid for by the club sponsor T-Mobile, and we've all been given Great Escape Survival Packs! Lets have a look what we've got shall we? A bottle of Ribena, a poster of the team lining up before kick off at Bolton, a card showing all of the remaining fixtures for the bottom four clubs, a Great Escape armband and last but by no means least, an inflatable pink T-Mobile glove/hand type thing! A Steve McQueen look-a-like (who doesn't look anything like the film star unless you're about 100 yards away, you squint a bit and it's dark!) was helping to dish out the packs along with the Great Escape T-Mobile Girls. These girls have become a familiar site at the Albion lately waving these huge pink flags at the start of each game and now there's the

Great Escape buzz, they're wearing camouflage T-Mobile tops and combats and bright pink coats! How much are they getting paid for this? Too much is the answer!!

Due to the fact that Andy "doesn't do coaches" and Paul wasn't that bothered either, today's trip will also be a Smith-less journey. Now I know the Fulham game was during a crap stage of the season (and in the end they chose wisely not making the journey) and due to the unfortunate timing of the re-arranged Chelsea game but come on, free coach travel, we can all have a drink for a change and not forgetting the all important survival kits, what more could you want?

We stop at McDonald's on the Brummie Road where there appears to be more people standing in the drive-thru than inside at the counters. Sausage and Egg McMuffin meal, thank you. We try getting on the East Stand car park in one of the many spaces near the gates, "sorry lads, you've got to park in Halfords Lane if you're on the coaches, cheers" a friendly steward kindly informs us. After parking we join the crowds in search of our coach numbers, we're on number 22. Ah, 38, 37, 36, 35, 34, 12,...16, what? Who sorted these numbers out? Oh yeah, the Albion of course! We find our coach and unfortunately have made it too late to sit next to each other. Stef's next to this vertically challenged bloke (politically correct – nice) who is not at all communicative and hasn't really been near a bath or shower for a while! My seat isn't much better though, I seem to have found the only other mute Albion fan and I'm right behind the toilet! To make matters even worse, the catch on the door is knackered therefore providing a constant banging and that delightful stale smell! I wouldn't mind but no one's been in there yet!

After what seems like a few hours on the road, or is that because I've been asleep and we've been "punished" by watching the Baggies Travel Video courtesy of Dave Holloway and his mate John Whats-his-name, we arrive at the service on the M25 shortly after leaving the M1. "Back on the coach in half hour please folks" is the cry from the front of the coach. Is this a school trip or BB summer camp or something? As we invade the services, literally, there's a decision to make. Do we head for the food or the toilets? Not necessarily because we're in need of one more than the other but because there's about 1,200 people all thinking the very same thing! I bet the shop assistants must have shit themselves! Profits will probably have hit rock bottom with the potential for a bit of half-inching. I was standing by a couple of coppers who had obviously stopped for a quick break, while on duty too (no offence Stu or any other PC's reading this) and were not aware of what was going on. They just stood there in amazement as wave after wave of these striped or red football tops came flooding past them! I went for the food option while Stef took the toilet route. A quick role reversal and I found myself queuing, yes ladies, a gent queuing for the toilets at a service station! Back on the coaches for the remainder of our journey. Ali G is now in the video for our pleasure, but it is cut short due to a complaint from a bloke who has brought along his young sons and their mate (I think). Fair enough, these kids are aged about 6 or 7 and I wouldn't like them watching it if I was their dad. He is hilarious but not for that age!

Our convoy of coaches arrive in the vicinity of Charlton's ground in what must have been record time. Having left the Albion at just after nine o'clock, stopped at the services for half hour, and now arrived at our destination, its only 12:15 – rapid! Let's find a pub! We don't get here this early in the car! Past the pub where we drank last time we were in these parts – too busy already – and further up past the station. Unfortunately there appears to be a lack of pubs further up the road, as we return towards The Antigallican Stef notices a social club allowing Albion fans in! "NO AWAY SHIRTS AFTER THE GAME" says the sign in the window. Well it's before the game now and we're not wearing Albion tops anyway! Two quid entry on the door, now you know that is definitely going straight into somebody's back pocket. Now this place isn't the worst bar we've been in but it isn't far off! Shitty little stage in the corner with some ropy looking curtains, horrible vinyl covered chairs and tables round the edge of the room and a wooden dance floor area in the middle which is completely empty, I don't mean that there's no one dancing, I mean no one's on there cause you'd have to stand there like a dick and you'd be blocking someone's view of the footy. Sorry, Yeah, forgot to mention they'd got footy on a big screen – Scottish 2nd division or something crap but you've still got to watch it, haven't you? We decide to prop against a ledge next to the fire exit. After a few bottles of Becks or Bud, we venture to the outer area of the beer garden, or should I say, a fenced off area of the car park with a reel of barbed wire round the top of the perimeter fence – I know we're on about the Great Escape but this is ridiculous.

In the rear "lounge" there are even more of the hideous chairs and even more tables, Albion fans and Charlton fans mingling and chatting with each other before the "fun" begins. They've got the football on in this room too, but it's on a 21 inch TV which looks like it gets wheeled in on a trolley for special occasions. Right, enough of taking the piss out of the social club, we're moving onto the ground now. As we follow the crowds towards the ground there's a quick chance of heckling Gibby and his crew who have decided to go for the cans-out-of-a-carrier-bag-outside-the-offy pre-match drink rather than the more "sophisticated" social club! If I remember rightly, last time when we came here it must have been around Christmas time because it was on a Saturday but I just remember the ground being in darkness, either that or it was absolutely pissing down at the time. Today in the bright sunshine, the ground does look quite impressive, apart from the away end! There are still girders blocking your view if you're unfortunate enough to be sitting in the upper tier. This time we're sitting half way down the lower section so should have a good view of most of the game and a great view of any goals at our end.

Ronnie could have and should have put us one-nil up after only a couple minutes but his drive was well held by Kiely – sorry lads, not the babe from Down Under - in the Charlton goal. Greening is playing real-ly well out on the left, taking blokes on and putting in some good cross-es. Gera is up to his usual stuff on the right; beating one, cutting inside, shooting wide or over! Never mind, it's all good stuff, Charlton haven't really threatened so far and they're going for a UEFA spot too! Another great cross from Greening is half cleared, well, up in the air by the Charlton defence. It comes out to Gera just inside the right edge of the box, a quick cross with the inside of his boot and the Horse is there to nod home into an empty net. One-nil after only nine minutes. Great! Fantastic! Brilliant! Manic boinging, shouting and waving of silly pink hands is met with the usual rendition of The Lord's My Shepherd. After Gaardsoe had almost let their strikers in with a weak header back towards Hoult, he was replaced by man mountain, Big Dave. Gera then curled a superb free kick around the wall but Kiely managed to keep it out even after a deflection off a head in the wall. Then a defensive error saw neither Moore nor Clem pick up Johansson and he latched onto a perfectly weighted through ball from the midfield. Hoult did manage to prevent his chip going in but it bounced back into his path and he easily made it one-one. Mark Halsey, who didn't have a bad game to be fair to him, helped the Albion's cause before half time by sending off El-Karkouri. There couldn't have been too many complaints though, the guy came in to challenge Gera with both feet and studs showing…oooh, I'm wincing in pain just thinking about it, he caught him all down his thigh. Nasty! Off you go! We could have gone in at half time a goal up but once again Kiely managed to tip round a curling effort from Wallwork.

Second half started as the first had ended. All Albion! No really, honestly, I'm telling the truth! Robson has finally got these guys believing in themselves and they can play some great football when they put their minds to it. Paul Robinson could have opened his Albion account and doubled his tally in the space of about ten minutes at the start of the second half. He shot narrowly wide after more good work from Greening and then Campbell put him through with a clever ball but this time Kiely took hold of his well-struck shot. Then another 20-yard effort from Gera almost skimmed off the woodwork. Richardson made way for Earnie with half hour to go, I don't think Robson took him off because he was playing badly, not at all, I just think we needed an extra direction up front and Earnie's extra pace could well upset the big-guys at the heart of the Charlton defence. Bartlett had two chances to take the home side in front but Robinson did well to get back and clear the danger. More Albion pressure then gave Earnie the chance to take us into the lead. Robinson crossed a deep ball into the area where Horsefield was on hand to nod the ball back across goal for Earnie to nod home unchallenged. Cue more boinging, cheering and those pink inflatable hands!

Earnie's second and Albion's third put an end to our worries and concerns about hanging on for 15 minutes or so and then in true Albion style letting the opponents back into the game. Since Robson and Pearson have managed to put together their strongest Albion 11 or so players, they have managed to get them to carry on attacking and go for the outright winner. No disrespect to previous managers, but at this level, as we've already seen on more than one occasion this season, any team can pinch a goal out of absolutely nothing and ruin it for everyone! In the lower leagues you may get more chances on goal per game but people just don't seem to have the same eye for goal like Premiership strikers. In this league if you give teams a chance, 9 times out of 10 it's in the back of the net! In previous seasons we would have took the lead and then shut up shop, or tried to, usually enduring at least 10, 15 even 20 minutes of nail biting agony and calling for the final whistle with 5 minutes still on the clock! This goal came from an exquisite ball from Gera along the floor, from just inside the Albion half, to Earnie. It split the defence completely and left Earnie to home in on goal, one on one with the keeper. From just inside the area he made sure with a delightful shot into the opposite top corner. Cue even more boinging, more cheering and the inevitable hands. Six minutes left and job done. Well done Robbo, another masterstroke in the art of substitutions timed to perfection. If I were you, I'd give Chaplow a run for the last few minutes. Not sure if he heard me but guess what, Chaplow is given a run out for the last few minutes. Now I know he hasn't started yet but if his first few touches are anything to go by the Albion should give him a contract for life! Not sure who played the ball up to him but he got the ball on the edge of the box, twisted past one, turned another inside out then cut it back along the touchline before being hacked down by a pissed off (probably) Hughes. Definite pen! Guess who grabbed the ball first? Yep, Earnie. Well you can't blame him can you really? A hat trick at every level he's played professional football at. I'm not sure how many more chances he'll get to score a hat trick in the Prem so here goes, calm as you like, sending Kiely the wrong way. Get in there! A very convincing 4-1 victory against a team with a chance of finishing in Europe – not after today he he he – surely we have proved to people we have moved on a great deal under the new leadership team now?

We leave the ground amid scenes of such joviality that anyone would think we have won the league, let alone started the enormous task of getting out of the relegation zone. It reminded me of the scene at the end of Fever Pitch when Arsenal have won the double and everyone is out in the streets. We're a very, very big distance from winning any double but it sounds good doesn't it – maybe one day! We reach the coaches and after a struggle to find our numbered vehicle, we take up our seats and after cheering the results on Five Live settle down for a few hours kip on the way home. I think Mr Peace should have another word with T-Mobile, this free coach lark seems like a winner. What's the next away game, after Everton at home? Villa! Think we'll need tanks and armoured jeeps instead of coaches for that one!

Everton home

Now some people are thinking the unthinkable - we could stay up. Premature I know but winning games has that effect on you I'm afraid. We haven't got another game on a Saturday at 3pm for the rest of the season home or away - TV nation. Now Everton have been in the top 4 all year, no I'm serious, all year. Not since the days of Gary Lineker have the Toffees been this high up the League. In fact, for the past 10 years they have fought off relegation to be honest and cheated relegation actually - Hans Segers, Wimbledon, last game of the season, had to win, 2 - 0 down, came back to win 3 - 2 after Segers dived over the ball in the final few minutes and since got accused of match rigging. I tell you, the team that got relegated that year in place of Everton must be devastated. Anyway, their team is no better than most of the ones that struggled in the past to be honest but Moyes has instilled a bit of spirit and fight and they win 1 - 0 regularly. They are similar in style to Bolton but don't get the bad press. I hadn't been impressed with them once all year so saw this as a fixture we could genuinely have hope in.

We kicked off at 4pm because of Sky, so played footy in the morning and went to the George for a quick drink before the game. I was man of the match again, which is getting a bit boring so we talked about something else. (I know you're laughing now lads). We parked up and walked up the road and as I waited to cross, two coaches came round the corner with loads of Everton fans on board. As I waited, one little scally with the customary shaven head and tracksuit top done up to his neck stood up and showed me his middle finger while mouthing wxxker. That's nice I thought. We made it to the ground in plenty of time and had a bet before kick-off. Robbo started with the same team that began against Charlton at the Valley last week, which meant hat-trick hero Earnie remained on the bench! Exciting Everton, who were looking to cement 4th spot and Champions League qualification ahead of rivals Liverpool, played one striker up front on his own and packed the midfield. Their fans sang about their history, which is all many of us have left to argue about thanks to Chelsea, Arsenal and Man Utd but they didn't sing about much else considering the football was so dire. It was 0 - 0 at half time with little in it to be honest, although I thought we had the better of things in a scrappy affair. I looked across at the boxes where Sky were and could easily make out that bloke off the Goonies, oh what's his name? Oh yeah I remember .. Iain Dowie. I still haven't forgotten his celebration on our pitch in front of the Smethwick End when we gifted them an injury time equaliser after scoring only seconds before ourselves - mong.

Second half was a little better. We played far more attacking football than the Toffees and deserved to be in front - but we weren't, which has always been our downfall. Then on the hour mark the ball broke down our left and Greening swung it over. Gera, our little mighty Magyar stole in at the back and leaped to head it down and in, past Martin. We went wild in celebration. No noise from the Everton boys but Moyes did finally realise another striker was needed so on came Big Dunc. Now Dunc never fails to deliver. It might not be a goal or anything to help his team at all for that matter, but he never fails to deliver - headbutts, punches, abuse, anything like that from the big Jock. Everton went long and Dunc flicked. That was the plan of action for the last 20m mins. Say what you like, it was far more effective than the tripe they tried before his arrival. Robbo responded and brought on our own 'Big' man - Dave. He is enormous, don't worry about that. The Toffees huffed and puffed but in the end failed to blow our defence in. Don't get me wrong it wasn't the Alamo, far from it in fact and we really deserved the 3 points but the final few minutes were agony. Not helped by the strange choice of 5 extra injury time minutes. Nail biting, hair pulling, feet shuffling tension - any cliché you like. The whistle blew and we sounded our victory. I was so chuffed. I stood on my chair and looked across at the sorry Scousers, desperately searching for the finger dick from the coach earlier, knowing full well I wouldn't see him, I looked all the same with a big smile on my face. The Smethwick sang "Champions League ... You're havin' a laugh", which I truly believed in all honestly. We laughed our way down Halfords Lane spotting Toffees with their kagouls on upto the neck and shaven heads looking all hard - not.

Are we really going to do it? This Great Escape thing is picking up momentum I'm not joking. Our run in is still the toughest out of all the bottom 4 clubs but our form is picking up nicely if you don't mind. Can we really go down in history as the first club to stay up after being bottom at Christmas? One thing is for sure, if we do Robbo should be made a knight and manager of the year. Forget Jose big headeeyo, and all the others. I'm getting carried away now, I can sense it. The thought of next week is now starting to control my character - the Vile. Oh well, to the tune of Amarillo... everybody.... "We are on our way to Aston Villa, Zoltan Gera's gonna get the winner, take me back to Aston Villa, where Zoltan Gera scores for me".

Aston Villa away

The game of the season for me. I get palpitations just thinking about this fixture to be honest. Most people know by now that I simply can't stand this lot. I'm not one-eyed enough to disagree with their claim to be the biggest club in the Midlands because I suppose they are really. A clubs stature is based on a number of factors. I believe when you are talking about the size of a club you are referring to the result of a cocktail of history, honours, ground, support, financial clout and staff, including players. Until recently the vile led the way in all of the factors but the Blue half of Brum now speak loudest financially, which pisses Villa off no-end. Unfortunately for all the Midlands clubs the factor we hold onto so dearly is our history/honours (except for the Blues of course). Albion, Wolves and Villa all have reasonably proud pasts but that's just it - years gone by. Take away 2 years at the start of the 80s and the Villa's honours sit pretty amongst the Royal Engineers and Newton Heath in the 19th century, when you played 3 games to get to the Oval Cup final and 12 teams packed the league. Villa have had a poor season, they talk of Europe every year like its some God given right for them to be there but they are way off the pace. They have lost to the Blues both home and away and went out of the Cup to lower league team Sheff Utd. They have spent very little because they can't afford to and attract average players at best. Is it me or are they slipping from their top spot mantle? Let's hope so.

We arranged to meet Swoff at his house before the game as he was taking us into a pub he frequents behind the main stand. Now that doesn't seem odd but when you consider we kicked off at 12 noon and were meeting at 9am I think you get the picture. Gav picked me and the

Smiths up at 5 to and we headed for Swoffs. I was asked in to the Swoff household but Lil didn't make me that bacon sandwich she promised. We followed young Swoff to Villa Park and parked up. After sneaking round the back of the Upper Grounds we sat down together and supped our first pint Sunday morning at half nine! Swoff senior soon joined us and we enjoyed a bit of banter - "now don't get confused, you're gonna see a big ground today" .... "Yeah and you might even fill it now we are here" so it went. The atmosphere was good and I thank John for taking us there - I'll buy you some scratchings one day and a bit of cheese, sorry chaise as he says. We strolled to the ground in the sunshine and my butterflies began a merry intestinal dance. There were some charity box collectors outside the Trinity road - " I see Doug is trying to get another player lads".

We entered the ground after walking across the carpark beneath the North Stand and found our seat - right behind the goal, some way back. The Albion filled their section and the chants went up. As the players walked out my neck hairs stood to applaud with me and the occasion had me in its grasp. The memories of past encounters came flooding back, the Villa fans I know and love showed their faces in my mind - Moog, Big Mart, Dai, Bob, Small, Big Summers, Gurp, Richie Stevens, Big Craig, Wardy, Sully and many others. For the next 90 mins I wanted nothing in the world more than to see the Albion turn them over.

The game started and we didn't. Villa controlled midfield, which annoyed me to the point of bursting considering they had that annoying little Chav Lee Hendry in there with a young kid along side him. We had Richardson, who just couldn't get started and the Rock - Ronnie Stalwart, say no more. They had a lot of possession without really testing Hoult and we just simply tried to break things up and get going ourselves. After about half an hour the ineffective Albrechson gave the ball away on our right which we scrambled away for a corner. The ball was swung across and 12million pound man (that is a joke, right?), Angel headed goalwards. Hoult made a brilliant reaction save and tipped onto the bar. Nobody reacted but for England wannabe Vassell, who simply nodded into an empty net right in front of us as Hoult was grounded. 1 - 0 Villa. My heart sank and all the negative thoughts of facing the 'music' came flooding back to me. We tried our best to get back into the game but too many players were having off days. Gera was poor,

Richardson being carried, the front two isolated and ineffective and Albrechson was awful (please don't ask how much we paid for him because I wince every time I hear the figure). Campbell should have made it 1 - 1 just before half time but he blazed over with only Sorryson (he says this every time he plays the Blues) to beat. 1 down at half time - come on Robbo do your stuff mate, I thought.

Second half we came back into it more. Gera was clean through but his shot was tipped round the post when I'm sure he would score. During one goal-mouth scramble the ball was flying straight to Campbell for a tap-in when Horsfield stuck out a foot and diverted it away to safety. It was that kind of afternoon. The clock seemed to be on fast forward. Minutes ticked away. I just knew time was going to run out on us. We survived a few hairy moments in defence but Villa were not the threat they were in the first half. Tempers flared as the young Ridgewell squared upto Greening. They put their heads into one another's face, then the young Villa defender moved his forward like a butt twice right in front of the ref. - Goodbye I thought. The red card came out and up went the cheers, the kid could have no complaints the idiot. Greening was then called over to get a talking to, well this is what I expected as he had done nothing. But no, gutless tosser Stiles preferred to even things up and sent Greening off too! Time ebbed away and our chance had gone. Lost to the Vile again. 3 minutes injury time was awarded when Gera had a free kick on the edge of their box. He curled it over and I thought this is it. No, it flew inches over the bar. There must have been 30 seconds left, the ground was half empty (faithful Villa right to the end!) when substitute Scimica was sent down the line on an overlap by Gera. He whipped in a beauty of a cross that was inadvertently flicked on by a Villa defender, the ball raced across the area and left back Paul Robinson threw himself at it. It met his head square and flew into the back of the net straight for me. I shot a glance at the linesman and the ref. in a split second then realised we had scored. The Albion end simply erupted. Hundreds filled the isles and spilled over the advertising boardings onto the perimeter of the pitch. I lost total control of myself and nearly smashed the chair in front to pieces. Blokes all around me had fallen over onto the floor. The Albion players were in a heap on the floor saluting the barmy fans. I looked up at the Doug Ellis stand to see a line of Albion fans cheering amongst the remainder of the home fans. The celebration lasted for an eternity and I for one have never experienced anything like it before. I stood on my seat with arms wide - "The Lord's My Shepherd" and my favourite in response to the Hoult Ends mimicking just seconds earlier.. "Shit on the Villa". I stopped singing this after about 3 minutes, sat down and nearly passed out. The ref. had blown for full time after 2 touches of the ball from the re-start. It was a truly amazing scene. Okay it was only 1 - 1 but we felt we had won the cup and they were devastated, I don't care what they say. One particular Villa fan just couldn't take it and was giving it big from the upper North Stand. He was calling us this and that and pointing down to signify relegation. I swear he was looking at me. We walked out into the street and within seconds he was there. He shoulder barged me all angry and hard, I turned and laughed in his face as he realised he was surrounded by Albion fans - prat.

The sun shone and I danced my way back to the car. What a day. Another point towards safety, just call me Steve McQueen and send me to the cooler.

Spurs away

Picture this - there are five games left after tonight's visit to the Lane. We are out of the bottom four by a point, Norwich and Palace fought out a 3 - 3 draw at the weekend and the Saints threw a 2 goal lead away against the Vile to lose 3 - 2! The beauty of football - one minute you are screaming with joy to see a team lose, whilst next week you smile smugly after they do you a favour by beating a relegation rival. We now had a game in hand on Southampton and the other two with a point lead. This week would be pivotal in our survival hopes. We were at Spurs tonight, Boro Saturday then at home to Blackburn the following Tuesday - 3 games in 6 days. We needed something from this game just to keep the momentum going but Spurs always seem to do us and our friend from the "Emerald Isle" always scores. Tottenham are still looking up towards Europe and seemed in good form after securing a point at Anfield on Saturday, so the visit of lowly West Brom was sure to be the perfect stimulus for continued strides in that direction.

The Albion started really well and created some good chances early on. We were playing some good stuff with Gera looking liveliest but I always knew we were vulnerable at the back to the pace of Keane and Defoe. After a corner on the half-hour mark, England's actual number 1 flapped a little and only partially cleared to Gera. The Hungarian hit it on the volley first time and angled a shot into the corner of the net. 1 - 0 Albion. We lit up the night sky and belted out our Anthem. Last time we came here we battered Spurs for 45 minutes in the Cup then got done by a dodgy penalty decision in first half injury time - we never recovered and lost 3 - 1 that day. With this in mind I knew how important it was to keep the lead till half time. We continued to play well and to be honest, but for a few Spurs' flurries, we coped well at the back. Half time did come and we were 1 up and looking okay - can you believe I'm saying that? I mean I am talking about the Albion not the Arsenal here. How many times have they kicked you in the stomach when you least need it? Don't answer because, well it's not needed is it?

The second half started reasonably well but Spurs looked a little more dangerous and it was no surprise when they equalised. The ball was not cleared from the edge of our box and who else was there to pounce on it and lash it home on the volley? Yeah you guessed it the little Dingle from yesteryear - poor mans somersault to boot. My heart sank and I just couldn't help but think there was only one outcome now. The rest of the game was to and fro with both sides surprisingly looking likely to score. I say surprisingly because even the Albion looked lively. The game entered that awful period for me and the rest of the faithful - the last ten minutes. We have lost so many points in the last minutes of a game it's just not funny. I am well aware that most clubs can say this but it is still fact - if we had played to 85mins this season and not the full 90, we would have about 12 more points and be in mid-table safety. I also know I've already said that but so what. My heart jumped a few times and I clock watched as usual but still the score remained the same. Injury time was now upon us, which to be honest, is just that to us Albion fans. It is a time when we get injured, I don't mean on the pitch I mean as fans. Disappointment after disappointment, hurt after hurt, you know - injury! Anyway the time actually went for a change and the whistle sounded loud and clear. Another point towards our survival - we are on a run boy you better believe it.

Pete Webb enjoyed his experience too....

Always fun travelling across London to see a game. Throw in a mix of rush hour commuters, London underground staff still waiting to attend their first customer services course on how to look after customers, and you have the perfect blend for an impatient unforgiving race of people.

"What's he doing for God's sake" as the queue lengthened behind me. Not yet mastered the art of obtaining a ticket for Zone 3 from a choice of two buttons; Zone 1 or Zone 2.

'Time Out' flashed on the screen just before the ticket machine shut down which didn't help matters, as the queue was then forced to break up and re-join another long queue. "It's not my fault" wouldn't have helped my popularity much so there was no point in attempting to explain that it was all the Ticket Machines fault. Just find some helpful staff to sort a ticket out for me.

Mrs Unhelpful in the ticket office would have none of it. "We don't go to Tottenham –just tell me where you want to go" she kept repeating. Do they send them on courses to be impatient and objectionable?

The 'free train' from Seven Sisters to White Hart Lane is a good idea, just a pity it's full to breaking point of Tottenham die-hards. Should have realised, just keep your mouth shut and no one will know.

Top marks for the pie and chips from the Greek chippy under the bridge – this makes up for all the hassle. 10 minutes of top class stodge and we are back to positive thoughts only about our chances tonight.

Good seats in the upper tier, some familiar faces in the crowd including Adrian Chiles to my left, but can't see how 3 seats width of orange safety netting can be described as safe.

Chaplow in for the suspended Greening for 'head-butting' Ridgewell at Villa – (I've seen more aggression from the choirboys in Songs of Praise) – but put Rob Stiles on the pitch and anything can happen. Greening will be missed – top player this year, but more importantly, no Rob Stiles to stop us tonight.

Bright start from Chaplow, creating chances with a delicate touch, the best of all for Kanu. When is Kanu going to take football seriously and score again? Still, tonight could be the night Campbell has a good game – we've waited long enough for it. Gera puts us 1 up, but should be 2 or 3 by half time. Baggies in control of the game however. Inamoto makes a first appearance too, on for the injured Richardson. I like his controlled two footed lunges, and he looks a good prospect too. The future looks bright. Three subs at half time from Martin Jol reflect Albion's first half supremacy, but where did that Mido come from? Far too dangerous for our defence, and soon 1-1. The Neanderthal's across the safety netting wake up and the security ladies don't stand a chance until the back up arrives.

The last 10 minutes at 1-1 don't seem so nerve wracking - we are at last able to hold on to the ball much better – and every credit again to Bryan Robson. After conceding 9 goals in 1 week at Christmas, to Birmingham and Liverpool, and Championship survival looking like hard work next season – his achievements in recent months look like:

• Just 4 goals conceded in 7 games – with the same players that Megson had!
• Mid table form, and points since Christmas
• A midfield that has genuine flair
• Skilled attacking football for the first time in 5 years

All of this is attributed to Robson – for the first time in the two Premiership seasons we are watching a solid, organised team with flair that is good to watch.

Another away point to European chasing Tottenham – just keep quiet on the return trip on the Football Special to Seven Sisters. I didn't stand out though, as neither were the Tottenham supporters talking – strangely quiet tonight.

Boro away

The "numbers" are dwindling again, things are not looking good, but we are taking another 40-odd coaches to Middlesbrough. That's why "our" numbers are low, not the Albion's numbers. Albion's numbers dropping? You must be mad, free travel again. All aboard! Vince will be joining us in part cause one of the blokes at his work had got a spare ticket for the game – which was nice - and one for the coach – which was even nicer!

After picking Paul up we park in Halfords lane and make our way to the East Stand car park. Coaches everywhere, hopefully in more of a numbered order this time, but today there's some more modes of transport on show. T-Mobile have done it again with the free coaches, but some how the Albion have managed to obtain some First World War vehicles to escort the coaches. There's a US Army jeep, a couple of personnel carriers and that bloke who still thinks he's Steve McQueen (and is probably getting far too much money in the process) has now got a boar war bike to sit on and pose for the cameras. He does look a right idiot in his T-Mobile camouflage t-shirt and his white socks – nice! All the T-Mobile girls were on hand as well, handing out goody bags and posing on the front of the jeep for more pictures. We're on coach number 7 today and manage to get seats next to each other as we're there in plenty of time. In today's goody bag we have a bottle of water, a poster of Gera celebrating his goal against Everton, and another inflatable pink T-Mobile hand. Accompanied with a copy of The Sun, with its Goals section and the Racing section (big into the gee gee's now these Smithies are you know) and FHM with the Top 100 women section. We were escorted off the car park by the military vehicles – I mean the Albion coaches were, not me and Paul because of our reading material! This should be a sight and a half going up the M6 with this lot in front of us, but unfortunately they turn back to the Hawthorns as we join the motorway. I wonder if we'll have a military escort at the other end?

After an invasion of yet another service station, our journey continues north, further north and even further north. How far is it to Boro again? No please don't answer that question! After we turn off onto the A66 past the new Darlington FC ground, the local constabulary pull the convoy over into a lay-by while we wait for the other coaches so they can escort us into the stadium. No army escort but it was a nice thought! Some of us get off to stretch our legs, the coppers check some of the coaches for cans of beer, and then we're all back on to carry on our journey. Meanwhile I phone Vince to see where their coach is. He says they're already there! I assure him he must be just passing the Darlo's ground. Same design – well they all are these days aren't they – just a bit smaller? No, he's pretty sure he's already there. And so he must be because we haven't waited more than five minutes and we're off again. Yeah, sure enough we're the last coaches to arrive on the car park. This, however, should mean we'd be one of the first few off after the game. We rendezvous with Vinny and have a quick walk round to where the player's entrance is. He says he's just seen Ray Parlour arrive looking anything but smart. Mind you he never was that way inclined was he, more like the Charlie Dimmock of football – and I'm not on about the chest region! We find our seats amongst the thousands of Albion who have journeyed north. Row 10, just to the left of the goal so a cracking view. I'm just glad AJ is still out injured because we're in his sort of territory for shots! Only joking AJ, but stick to your tackling in midfield.

We're on a good run of results at the moment since beating Charlton; we beat Everton, drew at the Villa (get in there Paul Robinson!), and got a draw at Spurs in a game we could have won. Now remember what I said about taking those chances in the Premier League. We started the game really, really well, in a positive frame of mind, playing some great football. Greening is still suspended from the Villa handbags and Richardson has an injury from midweek, so Chaplow has another chance to prove himself after a good game at Spurs. Ronnie and Scimeca make up the hard working, tough tackling, slightly too slow centre of midfield! Good football, simple passes, some good runs down each flank from Gera and Chaplow and Earnshaw could have, and should have, had a couple of goals within the first fifteen minutes. The most obvious miss was a header from 6 yards out which looked harder to miss than put in the back of the net. Another chance fell his way when Campbell put him through. Something tells me we're going to regret this if we don't start putting chances away – and I'm not just on about today's game! Once again it seems to be the Albion's season long problem needing 15 or so chances to get 2 or 3 goals. Boro haven't really done much in this opening half hour and their only real chance was a header wide from Jimmy Floyd Hasslebank. However, they still look far more comfortable on the ball than the Baggies (even though we are getting better at it!). Another attack is broken down by the home side and three or four passes later the ball is in our area. After a save by Hoult, Slizard Nemeth (what a name!) strokes home the follow up leaving the Albion defence looking at each other. No good looking now lads, just react quicker next time! A few minutes later, Nemeth breaks down the Albion right, outfoxes Albrechtsen and crosses for his strike partner Hasslebank. Hoult appears to flap at the cross rather than catch it or punch it and even though Hasslebank gets the final touch, it would have ended up in the net. Then to really put the icing on the Middlesbrough half time cake, Nemeth scores again. So let's just go through that again shall we. Albion have created some good chances and a couple of great chances and still haven't scored. Boro on the other hand have created four chances and have scored three of them! Need I say more?

The second half was really a non-performance from both teams to be perfectly honest. Boro had already done the damage in the first half and seemed happy enough to just keep possession and hit us on the counter attack on the rare occasions when we did get near the goal we were supposed to be attacking! It was one of those strange games where we could still be playing now and we still wouldn't have scored. Nothing was going right for us and everything was going right for them. Even Kanu coming on for Chaplow didn't manage to ruffle the defensive feathers enough to create anything special. For me Kanu is one of those players that you can bring on when you're two or three up and with his "crazy legs crane" physique and technical ability he'll get you another two or three goals. No disrespect to the guy but when you're three down, with ten minutes to go, away at "UEFA-chasing" Middlesbrough, he's not going to get you much!

To really give us a swift in the balls when we really had had enough, Downing was given the opportunity to send us packing with a Beckham-Savage-Anelka-whoever-esque free kick. Well actually it was a Clement-esque rocket, as he's left footed too, straight into the top right hand corner. Right that's enough punishment for one day ref thanks. Final whistle A.S.A.P if you don't mind? We board the coach for the long slog home. Non-stop to Halford's Lane – well at least that's something. Managed to stay awake the entire way through Ocean's Eleven as well, even if the sound quality was shit!

Who's next? Ah, Blackburn and the return to the Midlands for the one and only, Mr I-love-myself-and-I-know-it, Robbie "honestly, I didn't move because of the money" Savage. (That's got that off my chest.) A win against them should get the Great Escape back on the right track. This game wasn't exactly a derailment, more like leaves on the line!

Blackburn home

You know how I've been saying ... this is a game we really need to win? Well guess what? We were battered 4 - 0 at Boro on Saturday after enduring the silliest of ten-minute spells only relegated teams seem to experience. This was our game in hand. Palace have just beat Liverpool - you know that really pisses me off. All I've been hearing lately is Liverpool this and that in the Champions League... blah blah glory night at Anfield blah blah then they go to Palace and play like fools and get done. Well I tell you something, I hope Everton finish 4th now, so the only glory nights they have at Anfield next season involve a rock band or something. A few weeks ago Norwich were down, no really they were gone and then Man Utd decided to do a Liverpool and lost 2-0 in Norfolk. Since then, the Canaries have scored injury time winners in two of their last 3 games and now sit above the Albion. Only Southampton seem to understand that we need them to lose every game they play! Anyway, they are bottom with 27 points, we have 29 with Norwich and Palace on 30. 3 from the 4 of us will go in May and one lucky team will survive by the skin of their teeth - there are 3 games left after tonight.

Blackburn have gone from being a boring run of the mill team that didn't win many games, to a boring run of the mill team that doesn't win many games but doesn't lose many either under Hughes. They are not afraid to leave a foot in or elbow for that matter but then again remember how Hughes played himself? They have nothing to play for really after Arsenal brushed them aside in the cup semi but had just been to both Anfield and Old Trafford without losing. We still missed the craft of Greening but I genuinely believed we had enough to get the 3 points we desperately needed to survive. Robbo opted for Campbell and the Horse up front (pacey) with Ronnie in the middle and Chaplow out wide. We started reasonably lively and took the game to them early. Everybody's favourite long-haired Taff played at the centre of their midfield and soon got the customary boos he so longs for. Things were tight and I just knew it could easily be settled by an odd goal. We had a free kick on the half-hour mark some 20 yards out in front of the Smethwick. Clement, Richardson and Wallwork stood over it (maybe Ronnie was testing the wind or something). The young Man Utd loanee stepped up and swung it over the wall and past the flailing hands of Uncle Sam. 1-0 Albion - we went wild. The pathetic 200 fans from the North West sat motionless across the way and the Baggies stood to sing their anthem. It was a fantastic sight to see the whole ground with arms aloft, leaning back and giving us its best rendition of the Lord's my Shepherd. The rest of the half was back and forth with no more real efforts to talk of but Albion seemed okay with things, comfortable you know. The half time whistle went and we were still one nil to the good.

I sensed Blackburn would come back at us second half but still didn't see where the threat would materialise from. After about 10 mins, Hughes brought the Turk Tugay on in midfield and things slowly started to change. Our midfield started to drop back and we failed to get the ball out wide. Robbo, to be fair must have seen this and tried to combat their midfield dominance by switching Richardson to the wing, taking Chaplow off and bringing on Scimica to play alongside Ronnie. Not exactly the most positive move I have ever seen to be honest. We dropped back even further and seemed scared to death to go forward. Gera went missing and the front 2 were isolated. 2 minutes after the substitution and the Aussie Emerton broke onto a free ball that came across the Albion area. He chipped his shot high into the roof of the net to make it 1 - 1. It had been coming, no doubt about that, but you're never ready for it are you? I still felt sick and watched Savage celebrate with a piss taking smile across his face. Only seconds before, Clement should have made it 2 - 0 with a free header but he headed down and wide with the goal gaping. Blackburn now played with even more confidence and renewed vigour and we slipped further and further into our worried little shell. I watched as our season began to disappear in front of my eyes. The Steve McQueen music, the big pink hands, the optimism from that sunny day at Charlton and the euphoria from Villa Park became distant and transparent. We were staring down the relegation barrel because most Baggies knew this was our only real chance. Of our last 3 games, 2 were against Arsenal and Man Utd, which basically meant we had tonight then Pompey last game to get any points. 6 might just be enough most felt but any less certainly would not. I looked at the clock and knew it wasn't to be, the sand in our glass wouldn't stop, as it began to cover our heads, ready to take our last Premiership breath. The final whistle went and we had just one point. We moved above Norwich on goal difference but remained in the bottom three. Arsenal next, then a trip to Old Trafford - if Norwich and Palace get 3 points from their next 2 games we've gone. Palace have got Newcastle then Southampton and Norwich have got Blues and Southampton too.

It doesn't look good and only the most one-eyed fan thinks there is still a chance. I'm not being negative or anything but realistically it's over. I am 99% sure the trap door is about to open on us but I still get those silly little moments in my mind where we stay up because so and so loses here then draws here etc. etc. – sorry, just can't help it.

Arsenal home

For this evening's game, which is on Sky, we are entertaining the Champions. That's last season's champions, not this season's! This year they are bidding for the 2nd place spot with United, as both of them have been so far off the pace of this Premier league. Chelsea have been head and shoulders above everyone this year and thoroughly deserve their title. But enough of Mourinho's blue boys, we've got a job to do against the Wenger's reds tonight and then Fergie's reds on Saturday. What kind of a run in to the season is this?

Robson lays initial hand down with three at the back, Clement, Moore and Gaardsoe; four across the middle, Robinson, Richardson, Wallwork and Albrechson; and three up front, Greening, Campbell and Gera. Some would say that was a brave formation to play against Arsenal, even though we are at home but we need goals and more importantly points! It may seem an attacking formation but it is equally as defensive if you look at each player. Robinson and Albrechson will push forward with the best of them but they will first and foremost be defenders. Greening and Gera too are very attacking players but will track all the way back to goal if they have to. No disrespect to Kanu and Earnshaw but they are definitely attacking players. Kanu especially, would always prefer to create chances rather than prevent the opposition from doing so. Fair enough, that's what he's good at but tonight you just know that Arsenal are always going to have something up their sleeve when you least expect it – he of all people should know that, he caused the most havoc when he was there!

A couple of free kicks must have had the visitors worried as Richardson enabled Gera to show off his acrobatics and then took it on himself to curl one just over. Arsenal then started to take charge of proceedings. Vieira fired a long-range effort over the bar and then Hoult managed to smother a chance from Van Persie, after he had been threaded through by Silva. Ronnie could have and should have scored just before half time when some good work by Gera on the right enabled him to shoot just over from the edge of the area. After the break, Robinson and Clement both had chances to open the scoring but both failed to hit the target. Come on Albion, take these chances while we can. Who knows what's going to happen before the end of the game and next it's a trip to Old Trafford where we probably won't get many chances either! After an hour or so, as the Gunners grip on the game tightened, the inevitable happened! Van Persie received the ball on the edge of our box, wriggled free of his marker, created some space and then curled a shot into the bottom corner of Hoult's goal. Great!!! Just what we didn't need! Then Reyes raced clear, managed to evade Hoult's challenge on this occasion and directed the ball towards the unguarded net. Fortunately Clement was on hand to clear the ball off the line. Arsenal then showed the real difference between the two teams. Not a difference necessarily on the pitch – personally I don't think they have played that well tonight and Albion have fought bravely and nearly matched them in all departments – the real difference is in the squad of players. Arsenal have Bergkamp, Edu and Campbell to bring on if required and Albion have Horsefield, Kanu and Earnshaw! Again, no disrespect to any of them but they don't even come close to the huge international stars of Arsenal these days. Who knows though; if we do manage the unthinkable, maybe Robson will be able to attract the eyes of the bigger fish who may wish to have more first team football in the last few years of their careers. There's always hope!

Bergkamp and Edu are introduced shortly before Clement produced the kind or run you'd normally see from the Arsenal subs. Running straight out of defence, he was unchallenged through the midfield and left to run towards the edge of the Arsenal box. After a last ditch challenge, the ball found its way to Richardson who struck a fierce shot straight, unfortunately, at Lehman. In the last few minutes, the three Amigos were thrown on from the Baggies bench, but it was Reyes who almost sealed the result for the Gunners. As he danced his way into the box, Big Dave pulled off the tackle of the game to deny a certain goal scoring opportunity. As hard as the improved strike force tried, they were unable to break down the Arsenal rear guard. With the Albion pressing ever forward, it was giving Bergkamp the chance to show his higher class. After some delightful touches, he dinked the ball forward into the path of the advancing Edu. The inch perfect ball from Bergkamp gave Hoult no chance and as he rushed out in a vain attempt to narrow the angle, Edu nonchalantly chipped the ball into the empty net. Brutal! We really don't deserve that but again, it's taking your chances that win you games.

Don't think that Albion haven't created any during this game or in previous games, we have, it's just that we can't get the ball into the back of the net. We didn't deserve the 4-0 drubbing at Boro and we should have won the game the other day against Blackburn. Like I said earlier, it's Man United next and realistically we aren't going to get much from up there are we? Still it will be a good day out, a chance to visit a fantastic stadium. Hopefully there won't be any silly "Yam Yam" plane songs this time. Last time when we sung it they genuinely took it the wrong way! If we sing it this time it will be to wind them up (I think it will be sung, don't you?). Then after the game, the ones who are singing it will get on the coaches and it will leave the rest of us to fight for ourselves when the United fans start to get nasty.

We're still bottom and depending on results on Saturday, United could actually send us down, as our game doesn't kick off until 5:15pm! Another game on Sky!

Man Utd away

Man Utd away last but one game of the season when you're fighting for your life - that's nice I thought. Cheers for that Mr. Fixtures computer. We could go down this weekend. If one of the sides win in the Palace versus Southampton game then we must beat United in their own backyard to force it to the last game of the season. Put another away, if either Palace or the Saints win, we are down. Sky chose this game to go out live at teatime Saturday night after the other 3 sides around us had played. I don't know if that was worse or not to be honest. Surely never in Premiership history have we gone into the penultimate game of the season without knowing who is to be relegated from the league. Norwich have 30 points, we have 30 points, Palace and Southampton have 31 a piece. 3 from that 4 will perish. Palace host the Saints today, believe it or not and Norwich are at home to struggling Blues. Now you can see why I'm really grateful to the fixture computer!!

Last time the boys went to the Theatre of Dreams it turned into a bit of a nightmare off the pitch to be honest. Gav got thumped and split from Vince, both Smiths took loads of abuse and pockets of violence erupted everywhere. This was the result of some basic naivety on the Albion's behalf. When we play the Blues they always do an aeroplane impression and sing yam yam to the dam busters theme to mimic our Black Country roots. The Albion took a bit of a liking to this taunt to be fair and started doing it at away grounds sporadically it has to be said, from then on. First game of the season 2 years ago at Old Trafford in the sunshine seemed like the perfect occasion to remind a once regular, but now distant opponent of our accent's origin. Little did the majority of Albion fans realise but an aeroplane impression at Man Utd, considering the poignancy of Munich 1958 was simply not done. To say their fans were pissed off was the understatement of the year. Since then, feelings between the clubs have not been great. The home game that season saw fighting at the Blue Gates in Smethwick and similar fracas ensued after the League Cup game at the Albion last year. That said, we viewed this game with some trepidation.

Malc did his customary away fans guide and sent us along an A then a B road off the M56 to two pubs of our choice, as the pub closest to the ground was quite simply a big no - no. We followed the McHenry guide and found the closer of the 2 pubs by about 2pm. The carpark was chained off but as I approached it a bloke came to my window. I asked how much but he spotted the twang straight away. Sounding like Liam Gallagher he whined "sorry mate are you West Brom, well you can drink in here but you can't park here know what I mean like?" - no not really but we moved on all the same. He sent us round the corner and we parked on the wasteland by the Trafford Bar station. The pub seemed okay to be fair and we mingled in with the Irish Cockneys trying to watch the results of the other games. Palace and the Saints remained 0 - 0 for 30 minutes or so then the Eagles went one up. We desperately needed this one to end in a draw if we had any real chance of survival so for Palace to go in front at home against the struggling Saints was not ideal. 2 mins later, however and the hideously named Crouch levelled for Southampton - nice touch. On the stroke of half-time news filtered through of a goal at Norwich - penalty to the Canaries and Blues were down to ten men. Thanks a lot Blues that's just what we need!

We sank a few more beers and headed for the ground at about 20 past 4. Norwich were still beating the Blues and it was still 1 - 1 between Palace and Saints. Say what you like about Manchester United but what a stadium. It towers with significance out of the former industrial heartland and dominates the skyline. We found the away section and headed in after 2 body searches. I had a bet - Giggs first goal in a 4 - 4 draw, don't ask! We found our seats and surveyed the ground around us. By now Palace had scored to go 2 - 1 up. This was not good news for us. The stand opposite us to our right, the North Stand I think, is ridiculous, Paul didn't even realise there was another tier above the two he could make out!! Impressed. Looking round though there wasn't much segregation on either side of the Albion section - just a thin row of stewards. Time ticked on and Palace were still winning, if it finished as 2 - 1 then we had to beat Man Utd to take it to the last game - as mentioned already, that was simply not going to happen. I looked at my watch and it was nearly 5 to 5, surely the final whistle had gone at Selhurst Park I thought. Then all of a sudden as my heart began to sink one of those special moments that only occur at matches at the end of a season materialised. A wave of noise came from my left and literally swept across the away section engulfing me as it passed. There were no players on the pitch and yet the Albion started singing and boinging like we had just scored. The whispers told me that the Saints had equalised deep into added on time in SE London - it was a lifeline, unbelievable, we were dead on our feet and now we had a chance. A jolly day out with an inevitable end now became one of our most important games in years in the blink of an eye.

Seeing the Baggies walk out that red tunnel along side Man Utd as equals, even if it might be for just a limited amount of time, made my neck hairs dance. Robbo had really gone for it. He opted for 3 up front with Horsefield separated from Campbell by Earnshaw. Now no one could say that was negative. Fergie rested some big names to be fair but their starting 11 still contained Ferdinand, Sylvestre, Ronaldo, Smith and Giggs with O'Shea, Neville and Kleberson. Not a bad little set of players! Anyway, we were battered in the first half to be fair. Ronaldo got booed predictably with every touch - I am sure most mindless idiots just boo because ... well "It's something to do aye it?" Needless to say he wrecked us in my opinion and even when he fell over he got back up and chased the ball down. The Baggies simply looked out of their depth as Man Utd passed and moved for fun. They started singing going down and were generally taking the piss so some sections of the Albion end decided to reply. Now as I said at the start of the chapter, the first time the Albion did aeroplane impressions all hell broke loose and it was widely accepted afterwards as a silly mistake. A repeat would simply be seen as out of order - intentional piss take of Munich. So what did a load of Albion do? You guessed it "Yam Yam Yam etc." aeroplane arms the lot. Funnily enough, the United fans weren't exactly ecstatic about this. Loads stood up to our left and reacted angrily to the closest row of Albion just across a little line of stewards for segregation. Same thing was happening the otherside, then boos echoed out around the ground from all sections. One thing entered my mind - if we keep this up it's gonna get lively afterwards again. A burly looking steward came over and asked this fat kid in front of me to sit down. He did a 3-point turn and spluttered "we're only having a laugh mate, it's just a chant". The steward told him to sit down as he was on CCTV, he continued to argue his corner when out of nowhere a bloke shot up and ordered this kid to sit down like your PE teacher used to. The fat kid sat down. I realised after, it was his dad; his mom was on his other side! That's how hard he was.

Anyway, the half wore on when Hoult came out to punch and land-ed heavily under challenge. The Physio came on but our keeper must have waved him off, claiming to be okay. After a corner, Smith stooped low for a header and went over from a perfectly fair challenge - free kick edge of our box. Hoult lined up his wall and Halsey was talking to a United player. Next thing I knew a huge roar went up - Giggs had curled it straight in, over the hapless Hoult. He limped into the net and ginger-ly bent for the ball, he could hardly kick it such was his pain. Funny, a minute ago he must have been fine when the Physio was asking the questions! Loads of fans around me gave him abuse - why didn't he go off? Oh well a minute later and he had but the damage was done, we were 1 - 0 down at Old Trafford and looking like a true relegation threat-ened side. We were getting murdered as they say, Rodney Marsh said a week later he thought United were playing down hill - nice. How we got to half time just one down God only knows, but we did.

Second half started and the only change on the field was Albion's Pole in goal. The pattern of play this half though seemed a little more "stop start" and saw the Baggies have a lot more of the ball (this wasn't difficult considering the first half performance). We began to pass it and move and get forward and generally have more of an influence on the game. On about the hour mark, a ball was played forward for the lively Earnie to chase. He seemed to leave it, however, for Horsefield who bust a gut to reach it. It was contested with the United defender O'Shea on the edge of the box, slightly towards the away fans. The Horse (nice nickname!) used his strength to lever O'Shea slightly out the way and he stole a tiny march on him into the box. The United defender realised the danger and pushed back to gain an advantage - big Geoff went down. The Albion demanded a penalty, O'Shea put forward his innocence and I watched the Ref. as time stood still. He ran over, whistle in mouth, looked at the challenge scene with a little stoop then blew, pointed to the spot and ran to the side. I couldn't believe it- he had just awarded us a pen at Old Trafford. The fans went barmy - that's both sets. Only 2 men have scored a penalty in the League at Old Trafford in the last 13 years, (only 1 has been given that's why!! Joke). Nice statistic I thought as I watched little Earnie grab the ball and put it on the spot. He looked confident, if there is such a look, ran up and chipped it slightly with apparent ease over the diving Caroll and into the net. We had scored, it was now 1 - 1. The away section exploded with joy and shear amazement to be honest, we boinged and sang the anthem like our whole existence relied upon it.

The embarrassment forced Sir Alex into immediate action. The hard-working Smith gave way to the fit again Saha, one of the best midfield players England has ever seen - Paul Scholes, replaced one of the worst - Kleberson and the Boy Wonder came on for the Boy Yonder - Rooney for Giggs. We had a little spell when I genuinely thought we were gonna snatch a winner, Kanu was felled in the box in virtually the same place as big Geoff but 2 penalties at Old Trafford - now I know you're having a laugh. As the half drew to it's conclusion I sensed the anxiety amongst both sets of fans and began to feel that emotion you sometimes get when you know what the outcome is going to be. Usually it's the last minute winner syndrome but today I just knew United weren't going to score. The last 15 minutes saw them pepper our goal but the Pole was outstanding. He pulled off save after save including the tipping of a Scholes 25 yarder onto a post and a flip over the bar from Rooney. Wave after wave battered our cliff but the coastal defences we had in place stood firm (the pupils at school will grill me for that sentence). It was to be our day. Mr Halsey sounded his whistle after only 3 mins of injury time and we had secured a point at the Theatre of Dreams, which kept alive our season till the very last day.

We walked back to the car heads down and murmuring. The aeroplane taunts still ringing in Red ears were enough to keep me in low profile. We drove home as happy as you could imagine and contemplated the following week's scenario. It will be last match of the season and 3 from 4 teams will go down. We were still bottom but only by 2 points. The Saints and Palace now had 32 points with Norwich on 33. Basically, if one of those 3 wins next week, we are down. But we are still in there, there is still a chance - keep the faith!! Listen to me - I didn't give us a prayer a few weeks ago!!

As this game was so monumental we decided to say it from both our viewpoints. I'll let you work out who wrote which account... ...

Portsmouth home

Judgement Day, D-Day, the day of reckoning; folks, this is it! I know I've started by saying it before and I'm sure Stef has too in recent games, but honestly today is the day! We shall start today bottom of the league, we were bottom at Christmas and as we all are reminded every week on Match of the Day, "the team bottom at Christmas has always been relegated since the start of the Premiership"! Well this is the Albion don't forget, and we always do things the hard way.

Even a win for us today will not give us the satisfaction of staying up. In a very strange twist of fate, and I can't recall another time when any team has required a scenario like the one we face today – promotion-wise or relegation – as well as our result being in our favour, we also need certain results in three other games! That's right, a combination of four matches culminating in a Baggies survival! Like I said, this is the Albion, we always do things the hard way.

Norwich are lying fourth from bottom at the moment and today they are playing away at Fulham. Fulham are going great guns at the moment having just beaten Blackburn 3-0 when neither team had anything to play for. Another twist here, Norwich haven't won away all season, wouldn't that be just typical if their first away win keeps them up! If Norwich win they stay up; end of story.

Southampton, third from bottom, have the toughest of today's games (out of the four of us) at home to Man United. Unless Fergie decides to rest the big cheeses before the cup final, I think Saints fans have realised this year will be their first relegation for 27 years – aaah, what a shame that would be!

Palace are currently second from bottom and are away at Charlton. Charlton are playing crap at the moment so I can see a possible upset in this "derby" game in South London. That little bald AJ will probably have some influence on the game, as he always does, hopefully it won't be a dodgy penalty that keeps them up. He has a knack of scoring those! Now if you're sitting comfortably I'll try to explain each scenario. This is the table as it stands.

	Pld	W	D	L	F	A	Pts	GD
Norwich	37	7	12	18	42	71	33	-29
Southampton	37	6	14	17	44	64	32	-20
C Palace	37	7	11	19	39	60	32	-21
West Brom	37	5	16	16	34	61	31	-27

If Norwich win they stay up. If Southampton win and Norwich don't, Southampton stay up. Palace will stay up if both Saints and Norwich lose or draw, or if their win is greater than a Southampton win. For Albion to stay up we need a minor miracle. We need all three teams to draw or lose as long as we can beat Portsmouth. Yes there's always a catch with the Albion. The three results in the other games will probably go for us and we'll end up losing or drawing against a side with nothing to play for! All week different people have been saying things like "I do hope the Albion stay up, they deserve it"- obviously not a regular watcher of our beloved Albion! "It will be a shame if they go down" – we'd only have ourselves to blame if we do. "If they go down, they'll come straight back up" – that's what the Wolves thought when they went down. Apparently the Portsmouth fans are going to raid the club shop sale before kick off and support us all game. I think this might have something to do with the hatred they have for Southampton. The fans will be crying out if they can give us a goal and send their rivals down but I don't think the players will be that way inclined – they've still got to go about the game in a professional manner. They've got some foreign manager now as well and he won't understand the rivalry too much, he's only been in charge for about ten minutes! We'll see, at least it should be a good atmosphere to finish the season on, one way or another.

After the point we earned away at United last week, there is a real buzz about the place before kick off. Plenty of balloons and inflatables are being thrown around the stands and I'm sure a few people will have taken up Ladbrokes's offer of Albion to stay up with odds of 5-1. I'll be sticking a Tenner on that and I think Vince has pulled out all the stops and gone for a big purple Twenty. That's a century back, fair play son! We take our seats for the final match of the season. I personally think that people should not have their radios with them today, not keep checking the scores on their mobiles and not receive any text messages giving away scores from the other games. I know it won't happen and some people will be paying more attention to the radios than the game, but I just think that we should get behind the players today and make sure we win. If we don't win we'll be down, so let's get the first part done with shall we and wait to find out the other results afterwards, that's what the players have got to do after all!

During the first half of the match on the pitch, it appears that Portsmouth haven't been given the correct "script" for today's events. They are passing it around far too comfortably and have created several chances where they should have scored. A few attempts have sailed over the bar and Cisse has had a couple of shots just wide. At the moment he seems to be running the midfield. Come on Ronnie and Richardson. Get stuck in there! It is a possibility of course that perhaps they don't actually want to win the game and in doing so may be helping Southampton get relegated! You never know! "It's a funny old game!" They may be content to have possession and create the odd chance to show willing. I'm sure if the Albion got a grip of the game they would have an easier afternoon than they think.

During the first half of the matches off the pitch, we will be informed from all directions. There's a bloke in front of me with an ear-piece in, the father of the little boy next to mom has got his radio, Hannah and Danny keep texting me and the people in the boxes along Halfords Lane have got Sky on the televisions. The first news to break is that Fulham are one up – oh dear Norwich! Then we hear that John O'Shea has headed into his own net – Southampton are now up, well fourth from bottom. Fletcher equalises for United but on goal difference Southampton are still ok. Charlton take the lead at the Valley and just afterwards Norwich go two down. I think they can safely say they are down now – never mind eh? Poor Delia - Where are ya'? Or more to the point, where will you be next season?! Now where was I, oh yes, Norwich down and at the moment Saints up. As it stands:

	Pld	W	D	L	F	A	Pts	GD
Southampton	38	6	15	17	45	65	33	-20
Norwich	38	7	12	19	42	73	33	-31
C Palace	38	7	11	20	39	61	32	-22
West Brom	38	5	17	16	34	61	32	-27

The second half of the games produced the most twists and turns. Fulham extend their lead to three, Palace are still losing and when we hear that Ruud Boy has put United in front, chants of "we only need one goal" start around the ground. Cue Captain Marvel for another defining moment in substitutions. Horsefield comes on to replace Greening. He's played ok but not as good as some games this year and more important-ly "we only need one goal!" A cross comes over from Gera and finds its way to the Horse at the back of the box, a quick strike with the right foot and its 1-0 – he's only been on 30-odd seconds! "Boing Boing! Boing Boing!" "Feed the Horse and he will score!" Wait a minute, Palace have scored but as long as they don't get another we're still ok. Another goal at Craven Cottage and then Charlton give away a penalty – idiots! Guess who steps up to score his 11th penalty of the season and possibly the goal which keeps them up? Yes, that bloody blue-nose AJ. Should have known really! I just hope it wasn't one of his dodgy dives which got the penalty! He scores. They're up and we're back down to the bottom! Shit! The whole ground goes strangely quiet and subdued.

With fifteen minutes left Gera slots a ball into the box for Horsefield to run onto and a clever back-heel enables Richardson to cut inside the defender and slot the ball into the back of the net. This goal produced one of the quietest celebrations I've heard in ages. There was still the applause for the actual goal but you could tell from the reaction of the player they knew something wasn't going to plan. Richardson continued his celebrations towards the Halfords Lane stand to ask about results else where and must then have understood the lack of Boinging from the crowd. For the remainder of the game the teams could have played without keepers or changed sides or anything really! The Portsmouth fans were all chanting "the shit are going down" – well they had done what they had set out to do (allegedly!). They were happy and content – Southampton were going down! At the moment we need a Charlton goal or we were going down too! We could have got a few more goals or even let Pompey score; unless Charlton score we are down!

Now I know I'd never kick a man when he's down but Fulham have got 5 now! Norwich fans must be streaming out of the gates – apparently there are about seven thousand Canaries fans, many of whom must be sitting in the Neutral seats – remember?

In the far corner of the East Stand there seems to be some cheering and general excitement! Have Charlton equalised? The bloke in front has got his head in his hands desperately trying to hear for any change in scores….. Nothing! I text Danny, he says nothing has changed. The cheers continue up the East Stand towards us. There was no reaction from anywhere else though. It all dies down again. Then some sections of the Halfords start cheering. Even the guys and girls in the boxes of the Halfords are cheering surely something has happened. No, still nothing from the radios and no texts from Hannah or Danny. Don't you just hate false alarms! Then yes, that's it, the goal we're waiting for. Charlton have equalised! We're back on top of the pile. Come on now just five minutes or so to hang on! Reports come through that Fulham have managed a sixth right on the final whistle. Hopefully that's a mammoth trek to East Anglia crossed off the list for next season. Southampton have lost to Man United so that's another epic journey, hopefully, we won't have to do. Come on Charlton! The final whistle goes here at the Hawthorns and I wouldn't be at all surprised if he blew up early – no one was taking any real notice of the last few minutes. We are far more concerned that Charlton don't do anything silly in the last few seconds. All the players are together near the entrance to the player's tunnel. Surely someone has a mobile or knows the scores to tell the players.

Then it happened! Probably the loudest cheer the Hawthorns has ever heard! The final whistle had gone in London. All the results had gone our way and for a change the Albion had carried out their duties too! We are staying up! The players are running everywhere; the fans are, as you'd expect, running everywhere. Within a matter of seconds the whole pitch is covered with fans wanting to congratulate the players. Horsefield and Richardson are carried high by the adoring fans. Now we get the usual announcements over the PA system. Please move off the playing surface so the players and staff can come out for a lap of honour to show their appreciation. Eventually the pitch is clear and the players come back out. Up towards the Smethwick End, past us, past the Portsmouth fans, all ok. Unfortunately, as they go along the front of the East Stand some people break through the stewards' attempt at crowd control and chase after the players. More join in and more and soon we have a pitch full of fans again. On goes the PA again, "Please leave the playing surface, this is for the players safety and the safety of their children" (who they have brought onto the pitch with them – why?). The players don't have time to celebrate in front of the Brummie End due to the fans, so start to return to the tunnel. More and more fans try to reach their new heroes. "Please move away from the tunnel area. Player's children are being squashed and some are in tears." Well I'm truly sorry to hear that but I could have told you it was going to happen! I'll stop going on now and get back to the celebrations. Mom and Kate keep saying we should go on the pitch for a photo "for the book" but it would just be our luck that a steward would decide to detain us! No I think we'll just savour the moment from up here. Let's just have a look at the final positions, shall we.

	Pld	W	D	L	F	A	Pts	GD
West Brom	38	6	16	16	36	61	35	-25
C Palace	38	7	11	20	41	62	34	-21
Norwich	38	7	12	19	42	77	33	-35
Southampton	38	6	14	18	45	66	32	-21

Right who's for a drink then! I'll just throw this bit in for the Loughborough crew but in this particular season little Ruby was born, Norwich were relegated, Forest were relegated from The Championship and obviously the Albion stayed in the Prem. Only one conclusion as to which team she should follow – ask her great Grandad!)

Portsmouth home

I nearly started this with the usual... Well this is a must win game but I don't really think that's needed. These are the facts of the matter -

Palace are away at Charlton

Norwich are away at Fulham

Southampton are at home to Man Utd

The Baggies are at home to Pompey.

We start the day bottom of the pile, just like we were at Christmas. All week I have heard every Tom, Dick and Harry give their opinion on who will stay up and who will fall. I have been through it over and over in my mind and after umpteen scenarios I still couldn't see it straight. I was convinced we would win but just could not perceive all the others losing or drawing. Me and the lads played footy that morning but I couldn't really concentrate, although I did hear one of the others describe my finishing as clinical (will get proper stick for that). I hurried home and showered in record time. After wolfing down beans on toast I frantically headed for The George. Conversation went around its own merry-go but concluded as normal - "God knows". A few beers did little to suppress the butterfly dance in my stomach. We left for the ground at 2 ish and tuned in to Tom Ross. It was a beautiful day - the sun beamed down a huge smile and I pondered that famous day against Palace ironically, a couple of years ago for it too was bathed in sunshine. We walked up Halfords Lane amongst a swathe of blue and white. I could hear chanting from the Smethwick and my heart began to beat in anticipation. Once inside the chitter chatter seemed so loud it kind of roared at me. I squeezed through the hoards and got some more beer. Vince and Gav were looking to bet as usual but I felt obliged not to back the Albion to stay up for superstitious reasons I suppose, they got 5 - 1. We reached our seats and the noise was deafening. I looked at the away section, which was packed to the rafters as it were and smiled at the

Albion flags amongst them. Yes, Pompey hate the Saints and if it meant supporting a team you were actually playing against to send your local rivals down well... needs must.

We kicked off to a wall of noise, it was electric. All four sides were urging the boys on from the first whistle. Within 5 minutes of the start, however, the noise slowed and then stopped. Southampton had scored. It was a sign of things to come - whispers going round from radios and mobiles. I wasn't too concerned to be fair because I just knew Man Utd would score and the Saints goal came very early - don't panic. We couldn't seem to get it together ourselves. Pass after pass went astray, we were trying too hard in some cases and playing with understandable pressure in others. A spontaneous roar went up - Fulham had scored against Norwich. I tried to do the calculations in my head but it hurt too much so didn't bother. Another non-Albion cheer went up - Charlton went 1 up at home to Palace, then the whole ground erupted - Man Utd had equalised against the Saints. As it stood, a Baggies win would keep us up - this was killing me. The thing was, as the half wore on, the other results were going for us but we were playing rubbish and didn't look like scoring. Trying hard not to sound boring, I said how bloody awful it would be if all the others lost and we failed to win. I said this about ten times. Half time approached and we still looked nervous and goal-shy. Fulham were now winning 2 - 0, Charlton 1 - 0 whilst the Saints and Man U were still 1 - 1 - the perfect set of results but the Albion hadn't scored.

The half time interval was painstaking - I even shared a fag with Vince. We couldn't reach the bar, let alone queue up to find out the beer had run out! Sky were doing their brilliant best to be fair, at keeping everyone in the world right up to date with scores and league positions. That sports centre channel must have been like a drug this afternoon. We welcomed the boys back out with a roar that sent a shiver down my spine. I know every club does it every week but the will to succeed today from the fans was hypnotic. Everybody I looked at wore the face of a tortured soul. I looked at people who simply looked back and shook their head slightly. They said nothing but I heard every word loud and clear. A cheer went up - United were now 2 - 1 up on the Saints, I felt this was enough I really did. Fergie would simply not allow them to lose again after the criticism they received after we took a point at Old

Trafford and Chelsea had given them a lesson. So this was the scene - Norwich and the Saints were out of it now in my opinion, it was down to Palace and ourselves. News filtered through that Palace had equalised which put them in the boss seat. We had to score, we just had to, our Premiership life depended on it.

Robbo sensed the need for a change and brought on big Geoff. The ball broke free down our right and Gera centred I think. It was flicked on and headed towards the back post. Horsfield was unmarked about 12 yards out and slightly to our left. He hit it on the volley sweetly. The ball rocketed under the Pompey keeper and the net bulged - it was his first touch. We were 1 up and celebrated, justifiably like it was Jesus himself walking on the pitch. Fans jumped, rolled, hugged and fell everywhere. I have never seen anything like it, I nearly fainted in that split moment of emotional mayhem I have described so many times. Now we occupied the Premier seat, we were kings. Pompey passed it neatly and looked reasonably solid at the back but they were never going to bust a gut to score, I could see that a mile off. I felt we had won our match now so all attention turned to the Valley. An uneasy feeling soon swept round the ground as news of a Palace goal came through like a proper punch to your guts. The euphoria of a few minutes ago was replaced by a gloomy silence. Palace were now in the clear and there was nothing we could do about it, absolutely nothing - this was the feeling that killed me most. After a nice interchange between the Horse and Richardson, we went 2 - 0 ahead but I didn't even leave me seat I swear. The cheers were muted as we realised we were to be relegated unless Charlton scored against Palace. Ten minutes left, Norwich were 4 - 0 down and Delia really was 'avin it like she had asked for on that infamous night. The Saints were still 2 - 1 down and out of it, we were 2 up but Palace still lead Charlton 2 - 1. It was awful. Then without warning, a cheer started in the Woodman corner and it seemed to make its way round the ground like a Mexican wave - Charlton had equalised... yeeeesss!! No they haven't... yeah they have definitely, it's 2 - 2, they haven't and so it went on for about a minute and I for one was getting savage. I don't think my nerves could take anymore. After a period of endless agony the fans agreed... Charlton had not scored, it was one of the worst feelings ever. Some rumour had swept around the ground, which lead to ecstasy, agony and bewilderment in the space of a 60 second period that lasted a lifetime.

There were 8 minutes left when I contemplated our fate. Nobody had watched the game for about ten minutes, all were mesmerised by radio crackles and mobile beeps. Then a moment occurred that will live with me forever. The whole stadium erupted at precisely the same time, apart from me it seemed anyway. Fans were jumping about like we had just scored against the Vile. Surely this was no rumour … What? What? Palace? 2 -2? Tell me, please God tell me? 1000's jumped around like nutters but I still waited for some sort of confirmation. The sensible talking bloke behind finished a conversation on his phone with a huge cheer - that will do for me I thought. Charlton had made it 2 - 2 and there were 7 minutes to go. Our game became so irrelevant I didn't watch it. The clock and people with radios now held my complete attention. Malc texted me and said the whole of St Andrews was Boinging for the Baggies and singing feed the Horse... now that's respect. We entered injury time and the anxiety and tension in the stadium could have powered a small African economy. Some sat down, most stood. Some jigged nervously and others stood looking at the heavens, in touch with a greater being. I rubbed my face with a nervous twitch and waited. The whistle went in our game to no elation at all. The players ran to the dugout in search of enlightenment. They stood around, we stood around, it was the worst feeling in the world. Forget exams, job interviews, the 3 - 2 - 1 Bungee even, this had to be the worst "waiting to die" type sensation ever. I watched in a trance and then that slow-motion feeling took over. Our players ran back towards the fans, a huge cheer went up, my eyes closed and re-opened, we had done it, the game had finished at the Valley 2 a piece. The stewards tried in vain to hold the masses back but it was no use. Before I knew it, the complete green of the pitch had disappeared and a jelly like mass of fans let out all their built up emotion at once. It was an incredible site. I stood and surveyed this carpct of joy and breathed a sigh of relief that carried more emotion then any scream I could muster. Matt Barr tapped me with a light - he had given me a cigar before the game but I refused to smoke it until the end. So there I was, stood on my chair, arms aloft and a hamlet blowing in the breeze. What a beautiful day.

Robbo himself came out and I for one gave him the biggest cheer I could. Here is a man who has to carry the label of Captain Marvel around with him in his managerial life after an outstanding playing career. The expectation of which would destroy some men but he has risen to the task and right at that moment he was the ultimate and nobody could take it away from him. 8 points a drift at Christmas at the bottom of the pile, everyone, including me wrote us off without a prayer. He never gave in and so here we are sunning ourselves in this moment of history. We left the ground after half an hour or so and drank into the night. This will never be repeated again, 3 teams from 4 on the last day etc - never. I couldn't have written a better script, wait a minute, who is that on that stolen German motorbike? True happiness but then again, it is only a game.

Epilogue

I've had some time now to calm down and reflect. To sit back and take it all in shall we say? Whichever way you look at it, history was made on Sunday and we were there. It truly has been an amazing season. Once again, following the Albion has catapulted me through every emotion you could conceive of. From the dark days of St Andrews to the hysteria of Villa Park, from the bewildering City of Manchester Stadium to the down right gut wrenching at Fratton Park. It has been quite an incredible ride, a ride that came to a halt on Sunday with the train still running this time. The Hawthorns station will still be a Premiership station next year after one of the most remarkable journeys in the club's history. I said I wouldn't do it again - every game and all that but something inside keeps winking at me. You never know - don't tell Fay, sshhhh. On that point I must just add here how happy I am to have Fay as my wife. She's brilliant. Anyway I just want to thank everybody who has made this adventure possible and hope to see you all again soon.

Albion till I die.

Stefan

The season in short

Best ground   Old Trafford (surely no-one sits in that stand by Neil Armstrong)

Worst ground   Selhurst Park (Dive, can't get to it, wooden seats)

Best Pub   The Archal, Liverpool

Worst pub   The Queen Vic Man City (we didn't even go in it .. "they'll shoot ya")

Best fans (home)   Portsmouth (Oh come on, what choice did I have?)

Best fans (away)   Norwich (great atmosphere), Blues (they sang for the Baggies last game of the season)

Worst fans (home)   Fulham, Blackburn, Charlton (not sure there were any)

Worst fans (away)   Arsenal (moan, moan, moan)

Best day out   Old Trafford

Worst day out   Crystal Palace

Best player   Steven Gerrard (destroyed us home and away)

Worst player   Diao (Blues on-loan from Liverpool, I swear I'm better than him)

Best food   Norwich (fair play Delia - stick to this though aye love?)

Worst food   Everton (still grey meat up there)

Best programme   dunno, ask Gav

Worst programme   see above

Best goal conceded   Liverpool (surely one from 8 was good)

Best goal scored   (Paul Robinson, Villa Park .. please!!?)

Best moment   close one between injury time at Villa Park and the final whistle last game of the season

Worst moment   seeing that bloke from the Goonies celebrate a Palace goal in front of us on our pitch

Player of the year   Gera, Greening and Robinson (can't split them)

Friends and acquaintances of the authors

The following list names all the people who have had an influence on this book, even though they may not be mentioned in it.

Mom and Dad Langford	Nan
Terry and Trina	Uncle Graham/Dad
Scouse	Burg
Moog	Kev
Richie	Dave
Dearny	Bart
Deano	Gary Williams
Fat Bloke	Big Mart
Macca	George
Cyrille	Richie S
Dai	Robbo
Bob	Roy
Graham	Dunc
Wardy	Gurp
Big Craig	Young Swoff
Sid	Darren Ainge
Bill	Ray
Chris	Maxy Boy
Freddy	Ray H
Small	Ste
Sully	Shirl
Charlie	Matt Barr
Neil Brittain	Scott
Al	Martin
Chris	Jim
Daz	Hippie
Big Jim	Ian
Baz	Jon M
Garry	Clive
Stu	Jonathan
Dean	JT
Jasper	Yvonne
Pants	Smudger
JH	Grandad
Bones	

Sorry if we have missed you off but there have been so many people who have influenced us in some way or another.

Thank you all.